INVISIBLY ill and LIVING with *Hope*

ROBYN DERKSEN OLFERT

INVISIBLY ILL AND LIVING WITH HOPE
Copyright © 2024 by Robyn Derksen Olfert

All rights reserved. Neither this publication nor any part of this publication may be reproduced or transmitted in any form or by any means, electronic or mechanical, including photocopying, recording or any information storage and retrieval system, without permission in writing from the author.

Scripture quotations are taken from THE HOLY BIBLE, NEW INTERNATIONAL VERSION®, NIV® Copyright © 1973, 1978, 1984, 2011 by Biblica, Inc.® Used by permission. All rights reserved worldwide.

This material is not intended as a substitution for medical advice. Please consult a physician before undertaking any changes to diet, exercise, or medication.

The content of this publication is based on actual events. Names may have been changed to protect individual privacy.

Soft cover ISBN: 978-1-4866-2627-4
Hard cover ISBN: 978-1-4866-2629-8
eBook ISBN: 978-1-4866-2628-1

Word Alive Press
119 De Baets Street Winnipeg, MB R2J 3R9
www.wordalivepress.ca

Cataloguing in Publication information can be obtained from Library and Archives Canada.

This book explores the different aspects of multiple sclerosis. As described clearly, it's a lifetime journey, full of obstacles that have been thoroughly discussed. Robyn makes it very clear and easy to read and follow. It's a mix of subjective and objective professional details that are quite enlightening.

—Georges Saab, MD

I can say with absolute certainty that this is the first time I've laughed out loud while reading about orthotic devices. A delightful read for anyone interested in health care and the intersection of functionality and style—or simply looking to chuckle over some well-placed humour about life with mobility barriers and sweaty feet. Thank you, Robyn, for such a refreshing perspective on health care.

—Andrew McPhail, CO(c), BHK, Canadian Certified Orthotist

Invisibly Ill and Living with Hope offers a refreshingly honest glimpse into the complexities of navigating life with multiple disabilities. Robyn's vulnerability sprinkled with humour and detailed descriptions invite readers to walk in her shoes, gaining a deeper understanding of some of the challenges and triumphs that come with living with invisible disabilities. Her teacher-heart shines through as she encourages curiosity and limits judgement, making it a must-read for anyone seeking to be more inclusive and empathetic.

—Shellie Power, Bachelor of Special Education, Executive Director of Hope Centre Ministries

Robyn's book is an eloquent and humorous look at a hard and complex journey. She offers beautiful insight into the ways that invisible illness impacts an individual and makes them feel so challenged in our modern society. Luckily, Robyn also offers excellent opportunities to ponder how we can support people better and walk alongside them in ways that are truly useful and validating.

—Julia Stoesz, Certified Professional Counsellor

With wit, humour, and honesty, Robyn points out the very real struggle between proclaiming the sovereignty and goodness of God while living with disabilities that change our lives. Having personally witnessed Robyn's journey over the years, I believe she has the qualifications to speak into this reality, sharing the difficulties of her life while also challenging the reader to better understand the world so many with disabilities live in. I'd highly recommend you read it to better understand the journey of so many.

—Al Letkeman, MDiv, Senior Pastor, Nassau Street Church, Winnipeg

DEDICATION

For Husband and Claire, whose unwavering encouragement made this book possible.

Kevin, I cannot write these words without welling up with emotion. You have always believed in me and supported me in every new dream I dreamed. I could never have dreamed you up, though. You have been an unimaginable gift to me.

Claire Bear, you have grown from a remarkable little girl to an extraordinary young woman. Thank you for being trustworthy, for your sacrificial love, for all the inside jokes (even some French ones), and for letting me hang out with you and your friends.

CONTENTS

Dedication	v
Introduction	ix
PART ONE: *Invisibly Ill: Health Hiccups*	1
One: Brain Pain	3
Two: The Big Diagnosis	17
Three: MS School	23
Four: Not My Favourite Rollercoaster	33
Five: Tired of Being Tired	49
Six: A Tale of Three Benefits	61
Seven: It's All Right to Cry	71
Eight: Bland	83
PART TWO: *Living with Hope: Persistently Persevering*	89
Nine: It's All Right to Laugh	91
Ten: #BabesWithMobilityAids	97
Eleven: Disability and Fatigue Hacks	113
Twelve: Old Dog, New Tricks	121
Thirteen: Perspective	133
Fourteen: More-bidities	147

Fifteen: Takeaways—à la Carte Menu	157
Sixteen: My Support Staff	165
Seventeen: Visible	167
Conclusion	169
About the Author	171
Acknowledgements	173

INTRODUCTION

What do you want to be when you grow up? Do you dream of a wedding day and your future spouse? How many children do you imagine having? Those are such happy subjects to ponder. But what about questions relating to the darker side of life? Which disease looks most attractive to you? When do you want to start living with chronic invisible illness, and how many of these sicknesses would you like? Many of us make plans, and we dream of answers to the first few questions. But how can anyone plan for the surprise of life-changing health problems?

My second bout with chronic illness stopped me in my tracks. I was twenty-eight and in the fifth year of what I thought would be a much longer teaching career when MS made an unsolicited appearance in my life. We faced an unknown future and a host of questions. How could I live a full and happy life when everything had just changed? How could I be the mom my unborn child would need me to be? Would I eventually have to face being disabled? I didn't imagine or dream any of this. What now?

This book recounts my experience living with chronic illness and the resulting disability. In Part One, you'll learn the particulars of each of four significant health challenges I've encountered. Part Two will introduce you to practical ways I have contended with these surprises. Throughout the book, you will encounter themes of hope, blessing, and community.

All in My Head?
I tend to take the lead when it comes to poking fun at my health difficulties. To bring levity to what might otherwise be a gloomy subject, I sometimes say facetiously that my symptoms are all in my head. But my unseen conditions are genuine and most certainly not a figment of my imagination.

The Big Four
In order of diagnosis, the following medical maladies have had the biggest impact on me:

1. Chronic migraine
2. Relapsing Remitting Multiple Sclerosis (RRMS or MS)
3. Clinical depression
4. Irritable Bowel Syndrome (IBS)

The revelation that I contend with headaches, which are frequent and severe, scores much sympathy. Most people can relate to having a headache, and when they find out about the intensity of mine, I'm often asked how I cope. When I reveal the *chronic* nature of my *migraine* headaches, even more compassion is generated.

Learning about my MS diagnosis seems to be a much bigger deal to most individuals, though. Multiple sclerosis is apparently a juicier disease. It's the kind of thing that garners considerable attention. It's a serious debilitating illness, which has resulted in many using wheelchairs. That puts assumptions and questions into the minds of others. Often newer friends will carefully and politely ask me to share with them how I got diagnosed.

Migraine and MS are terms most people are familiar with, and mental illness could join the pair. It's been better understood in recent times, with more people able to relate to feeling mentally unwell. This awareness has made clinical depression much easier to talk about. There's definitely a greater understanding of depression being more than just feeling a bit sad or down in the dumps once in a while. It's on the minds of folks who are mentally healthy, as well as those who experience a mental illness personally.

My fourth hidden ailment is also one that's experienced widely, and three letters could be used to describe it: TMI, or too much information. The condition is officially known by a different set of three letters: IBS, or irritable bowel syndrome. Rest assured, I am confident I can be delicate enough to not embarrass anyone, including myself, when I discuss my experience with IBS.

Although these health hurdles are experienced widely, it's less common for one person to manage all four. I tend to be an overachiever, and acquiring multiple invisible illnesses is an area in which I have unwillingly excelled. You'll be pleased to know that not one of my sicknesses is contagious, not from reading about them or from being around me.

Takeaways
By sharing about my "overachievements," I hope my readers will come away with tools to inspire them to take action. To facilitate this, I've included a list of "takeaways" at the end of each chapter. These are meant to share practical ways to

apply the content. Sometimes I'll provide insight into better health management, often applicable beyond the diagnoses I experience, and in other instances, I'll share advice about how to relate to others in similar circumstances to mine.

Structure of the Book
I invite you to use the headings to guide you to the segments that resonate with you the most. The first eight chapters, found in Part One, are presented with attention to chronology—you'll learn about my illnesses in the order in which they each made their appearance. Part Two covers various themes related to how I deal with and manage my illnesses and disability and how I have found hope amidst those realities. Jumping around will not likely result in any unwanted spoilers. Go ahead and choose your own adventure as you digest the material in the following pages.

No Apologies
There are a couple of things for which I make no apology.
1. I am Canadian. I was born into it, so an apology for my citizenship would be peculiar. Canadians are sometimes known for overusing the word *sorry*; the fact that I just revealed that I won't offer an excuse for being Canadian made me chuckle. I might embrace different spelling conventions than you. Probably the one that will stand out the most is the "our" ending on words such as colour, honour, splendour, et cetera-our.
2. Unrelated to my earthly citizenship, I believe I have a heavenly one. I won't apologize for being a big fan of Jesus. Following Jesus is fundamental to whom I am, and it would be impossible to relay my story and leave him out of it. This book is not a clandestine effort to push Jesus and my views on anyone. That certainly wouldn't be his approach. If you're offended by my doctrinal position, I absolutely respect your right not to embrace it. This is a medical memoir written by a woman of faith; it is not a theology book. I'll leave those publications to people much more qualified to address such matters.

Key Players
In the Acknowledgements section at the end, I'll provide a more complete list of people who have played pivotal roles in my story. But there are six important people worth introducing at the outset. Derksen5, or D5, is the name of the texting group that includes everyone in the family I grew up in. From oldest to youngest, these beautiful people are Dad or Daddy, Mom or Mommy, Marcia or Big Sister, me, and Corinna or Little Sister. Yes, I am over fifty and unashamedly

still call my parents Daddy and Mommy at times; I continue to look up to them, and they have my admiration and affection. You may prefer to call them Ron and Anne. To keep you from wondering which sister I'm talking about, I refer to them as Big Sister and Little Sister in the book—that's also how their contact info is entered on my phone, and I often address them with these nicknames.

The last two to join my team will receive the most attention, and you'll get to know them well. Kevin has been my best friend, lover, and spouse for over twenty-five years, and Claire has been our exceptional daughter for over twenty years.

PART ONE
Invisibly Ill: Health Hiccups

One
BRAIN PAIN

I affectionately refer to the chronic illness I first encountered as *brain pain*. I don't have much actual affection for headaches, but I can't pass up a catchy rhyme. When I look at my headache history, I can conjure up a number of mental images that point to significant moments and notable headaches.

Camping (Childhood Headaches)
Seriously? Childhood headaches? Yeah. It's real and as sad as it sounds. My earliest memory of having a headache is from a time I was camping with my family. I recall walking back to the campsite with Mommy and telling her about my head hurting. I was seven years old at the time. Although my recollection of childhood headaches is sparse, a dear child close to me can't tell the same story. She has dealt with relentless migraines for years and is an absolute champ when it comes to going to school—even when feeling completely miserable. Her headaches are undeniable, and most children and adults would find them reason enough to stay home from school or work. My vague memories of childhood *brain pain* fill my heart with compassion for her.

Oboe (Grade 7)
I have a sharp recollection of headaches in junior high. My grade 7 year saw me in a new school with an exciting band program. It fed the heart of this music lover, and I developed many friendships with like-minded peers. I began my participation in the band program in the woodwind section playing oboe. By the end of the school year, I was convinced a phenomenon called *stale air* was causing my headaches to increase in number and severity. Oboists may experience stale air due to the small opening of the double reed they blow into; as a result, exhalations may not occur completely before a natural pause to inhale. If the instrumentalist inhales while their lungs already have air in them, the air becomes "stale," and the player can experience discomfort and sometimes headaches.

Christmas Gathering Aftermath (Grade 8)

Another memorable incident from my adolescent years is related to an annual Christmas gathering. Every Christmas Day, my dad's side of the family met at my grandparents' house and enjoyed many wonderful traditions. These included the usual Christmas dinner feast, generous gifts, the singing of carols, the reading of the Christmas story, and many treats, with little-to-no adult supervision or intervention. This was one day when we as children felt complete freedom to indulge in chocolate and pop without seeking permission from our parents. Unlimited soft drinks were standard, as were full-size chocolate bars. The cousins had plenty of free time away from the adults; there really was no time to ask if we could have one more dose of sugar. Grandpa always made sure there was a "healthy" supply of goodies and faithfully stuck to the tradition of serving some key holiday favourites we all looked forward to.

After one such gathering, I remember lying in my bed with a severe headache, worse than anything I had experienced previously. The strongest picture in my head is of Mommy sitting on my bed beside me. She was there to comfort me, and I remember telling her I wanted to pray that I would die in my sleep that night. I couldn't imagine getting through the pain and ever feeling better again. I wasn't suicidal; I just wanted God to put me out of my misery and take me to be with him in heaven. This is a vivid memory. Based on where we were living at the time, I know I must have been around thirteen. I'm convinced my headache was the result of all the sugar and caffeine I consumed at the gathering. That headache still goes down as one of the worst I've ever had.

Unusual Medical Advice (Grade 10)

Near the beginning of my high school years, I saw a general practitioner who listened to me describe my *brain pain*. She had the diagnosis and a prescription to go with it. This doctor told me I had *muscle contraction headaches*, and it would be a good idea for me to marry a massage therapist. Looking back, that really seems like strange advice to give a teenager. Besides recommending a specific line of work for my future life partner, she also prescribed what I believe was naproxen. This drug is classified as an NSAID, or non-steroidal anti-inflammatory drug, and it's stronger than the over-the-counter NSAID, ibuprofen. I cannot remember being given any warnings about side effects, including the effect it can have on the stomach lining—something that actually caused an ulcer in a friend of mine. I remember sitting in the science lab and thinking it wasn't really making a difference and, thankfully, I didn't use it for long.

ONE: BRAIN PAIN

Desperate Times on a Band Trip (Grade 11)
High school brought many exciting band trips. On one of these, we were in a large venue listening to a concert. I had a headache so severe I lost all sense of reason and wanted to do anything to remove myself from the bright lights and sounds coming from the stage. I ended up lying on the cement floor in front of my seat until one of the kind chaperones advised me to return to my chair, as the floor was much too dirty to be lying on.

Forbidden Fruit Juice
During my grade 12 year, for six consecutive weeks, I experienced an almost constant headache. I had a light bulb moment years later while talking to a friend, who was also a mentor and later became my family doctor. She'd experienced severe headaches for many years and asked me if I drank apple juice or apple cider. She advised me that apple beverages can be headache triggers. That was a big aha moment. I'm a creature of habit and used to pack the same lunch most days, which always included a tall tumbler of apple juice and a sandwich with cold cuts. I was having apple juice every day, and I believe that six-week-long headache, as well as many others, were thanks to apple juice consumption. *Apple juice seems so benign, you're thinking. How could it be responsible for so much pain?*

Apple seeds contain a compound similar chemically to cyanide. Most people can handle the amount found in apple juice, which contains all parts of the apple—pulp, skin, and seeds. You'd have to ingest the seeds from an enormous number of apples for there to be any risk to your life. However, some special people are chemically sensitive, and for them, the consumption of seed-containing apple juice comes with the side effect of a nasty headache. You guessed it: I am special people.

1988 Silver Ford Tempo (Early Adulthood)
Eventually I grew up, but unfortunately, I didn't grow out of my headaches.

I met my wonderful husband, Kevin, in 1998. One day early in our relationship, I contacted him during the workday and revealed that I was having a hard headache day. It was my first year as a teacher, and I was teaching an all-girls grade 6 and 7 split class (no wonder I had a headache). When he found out I wasn't feeling well, he sprang into action and did what he's so skilled at—worked to solve a problem.

Kevin drove twenty minutes across town and picked me up during our lunch breaks. After I got into the car and we had driven a few blocks away, he gave me some water to drink and the dish of fruit salad he'd packed in his lunch. Next, he climbed into the back seat, tipped my seat back, and started massaging my neck and shoulders. Remember the doctor who told me to marry a massage therapist? I knew I had to lock this one down! We were engaged six months after we started dating and married exactly a year after our first date. The picture in my mind of the silver 1988 Ford Tempo, carrying my knight in shining armour, is a happy one indeed. It may have been a physically painful day, but more notably, it was a day I got a glimpse of the future I might enjoy with the care of a thoughtful and selfless man.

Camp Pain (Early Adulthood)
The next scene is also associated with my teaching career. Two months into my position at a new-to-me school, I found myself on a middle-years winter retreat in cold and snowy eastern Manitoba, Canada. Instead of enjoying activities in the crisp winter air, I was contending with a painful headache reaction to the beverage offered at meals, which came from unnaturally purple sugary powder. This is a prime example of what can happen to a chemically sensitive person; I have learned that it's best to avoid foods with artificial colours and flavours.

Making Cocktails in Our First House
A memory that has stayed with me is the intense *brain pain* I often experienced while Kevin and I were living in our first house. It was there that I came up with something I referred to as my "headache cocktail." This was a combination of medications, which included three analgesics (pain killers), caffeine, and one antiemetic (nausea treatment).

Although this combination was effective in eradicating the *brain pain*, with the numerous medications involved, it's not surprising it came with side effects. Both the codeine and antiemetic were sedating to the point where I wasn't able to stay awake. As a result, I only took this before bed. Caffeine is effective if used as a "one-off" solution; however, prolonged or irregular use of caffeine can lead to rebound headaches. Severe constipation from the codeine was the side effect that made this a short-lived solution and ultimately not one I could tolerate well.

Lessons Learned on a Massage Table (Adulthood)
Massage has been either a big hit or miss with my head. Starting sometime in my twenties, I sought out massage therapy monthly, or as frequently as our private insurance would cover. One of the therapists I saw reacted to my news of being a headache-sufferer by exclaiming, "Oh! Headaches and massage do not mix!" I learned from her the importance of massage strokes moving away from my head. This is the opposite of how massage therapists generally work, and I usually start my consultation with a new therapist explaining my preference. Massage still has

great benefits to me in relaxing tense muscles in my back and neck, which can contribute to headaches. These days, I go to massage therapy for reasons other than specifically seeking headache relief, although that's always also a desired outcome. And Kevin still gives me regular massages.

In a Tight Spot (Age: Twenty-Seven)

Dr. Bev Rutherford is one of the dearest people I know. When I was twenty-seven, she was my family doctor and initiated what turned out to be a significant course of events. You'll have to stay tuned to discover how that plays out in the next chapter.

At one of my appointments, she asked if I'd ever seen a neurologist or undergone an MRI. I had not. Considering I'd experienced headaches for so many years, she reasoned having a neurologist's input was the next logical step. She made the necessary referral. This was the first neurologist I ever saw, and I would eventually encounter two other neurologists with different specialties.

With great optimism, I attended the neurology appointment. Finally, I was seeing a specialist who would get to the bottom of the headaches that had plagued me for so long. At our first meeting, he asked questions to obtain a headache history. He then ordered an MRI to make sure there wasn't anything happening in my brain to literally be causing *brain pain*.

I arrived at the MRI appointment with a bit of apprehension. I have experienced claustrophobic moments in my life and come by this phobia honestly, as it runs in the family. I didn't know how I would fare being placed in this long, narrow tube. In the end, it went surprisingly well and was borderline relaxing.

My second encounter with the neurologist's office was after the MRI results were in. I was told the MRI was normal and that it gave no clues as to why I was having headaches. This actually felt like both good and bad news. The possibilities of what might show up on an MRI that would cause *brain pain* are probably grim realities. But the fact that it showed nothing meant I was no further along in getting answers and, therefore, possible solutions.

Labelled (Late Twenties)

It was around the time of the neurologist visit and MRI that my headaches were classified as migraines, and eventually I was said to have chronic migraine.

> Singular or Plural?
>
> The condition I have is chronic migraine, expressed in the singular as it's one condition. When you read "chronic

migraine," know I am referring to one condition, involving multiple migraines.

Previously, my headaches had been categorized as *muscle contraction headaches*. These headaches didn't seem to make the news in the same way migraines did. Now that I knew I had migraines, I felt that my headaches had escalated past my pre-adult diagnosis. I could tell people I had migraines, and they instantly knew the pain must be severe.

My experience with migraines has involved severe pain, food aversion, and extreme sensitivity to light. I would describe the pain as sharp and piercing, sometimes throbbing. I've rarely felt as if I were on the verge of vomiting; however, food aversion is common, with nausea often present as well. Sometimes the only food that appeals to me is oatmeal or cereal, which it turns out make great suppers. On migraine days, my poor family has to endure living in a house with dim lights so that my pain isn't aggravated further.

I often use a 1–10 scale for rating my pain, and it's been helpful for my family in understanding the severity of my condition. If I tell someone close to me, "The *brain pain* is a nine," they know it's a doozy, more like doozy-plus-plus. I don't think I'd be willing to hand out a 10 unless it was so bad that I'd be hospitalized. But the prospect of going to a hospital gives me a headache.

There are different types of headaches, and migraines definitely don't have the trump card for the worst headache ever. People experience headaches differently. Whether your pain is from migraine, tension (which I think is equivalent to muscle contraction headaches), or something else, I don't doubt it's real. We need to listen to each other without assuming we know how someone else is experiencing something.

> *We need to listen to each other without assuming we know how someone else is experiencing something.*

Prescription Medications

Having my headaches classified as migraines opened doors to new treatment options.

Triptans. Triptans are a class of drugs used to treat acute migraine flare-ups. Sometime in 2003, triptans became part of my medication rescue therapy (as in "rescue Robyn from the *brain pain*"). These medications have side effects, but they're not as bad as the pounding migraine. Like other headache remedies, they have the greatest efficacy when taken at the onset of a headache. This intervention wasn't available when I came up with my headache cocktail. The side effects from triptans are more tolerable than the treatment I'd been using previously, and the medication was more efficacious at dealing with *brain pain*.

Prophylactic medications. A migraine prophylactic treatment is taken regularly (usually daily) with the hope that it will prevent or lessen the severity of headaches. I've tried five different prophylactic drugs but unfortunately experienced intolerable side effects with each of them.

CGRP inhibitors. These medications are used both preventatively and as rescue drugs. For about two years, I took a prophylactic CGRP inhibitor, which I administered once per month by intramuscular injection. The extreme constipation that resulted made this an unsustainable treatment, and I discovered later that this response is common. Eventually, this therapy came out in pill form, which could be taken at the onset of a migraine episode. In this context, constipation hasn't been extreme. When it comes to treating an active migraine, this medication has the fewest side effects of any I have taken, and it's usually effective. I've also been advised by the headache neurologist that it's less likely to cause medication overuse (or rebound) headaches. I met this neurologist when Botox treatment became an option.

Botox. Never say never, because in 2015 I did something surprising. I received Botox; specifically, I had approximately thirty Botox injections administered strategically throughout sites in my head, neck, and trapezius muscles. I receive Botox every twelve weeks, as it's considered a three-month drug. I have noted that when appointments stretch to a longer interval, the old *brain pain* starts acting up with a vengeance. There's no claim that Botox will eliminate migraines, but like many interventions for various health concerns, there is the belief and hope that the treatment will reduce the frequency and severity of the negative symptoms.

Just because you have an appointment with a migraine neurologist doesn't mean you'll be granted Botox for migraine. I needed to go through a tedious process before being approved. I was asked to keep a diary, rating my level of pain every day at specific times of the day: breakfast, lunch, supper, and before bed. This was not just a matter of checking yes or no. Every day at the prescribed times, I had to stop, pause, and really think, *Am I experiencing any pain in my head at all?* Then I had to rate the pain level and record the details in the diary. With that standard, it was shocking to realize I have some level of *brain pain* almost all the time.

I was worried I would underachieve their standard, but I well exceeded the requirement of fifteen days or more per month with headache pain. I don't win a lot of challenges, but I came out on top in that one. Honestly, though, I found it sobering to realize how bad things had gotten. Needless to say, treatments began soon after this.

The side effects of Botox were minimal. We find it humorous that starting about two weeks after receiving Botox, I could raise my eyebrows only slightly, if at all. At an MS neurology appointment for one of the standard tests, the neurologist asked me to raise my eyebrows. I tried and then explained, "I've had Botox." Interestingly, the doctor didn't seem surprised that I couldn't make a traditional surprised face, and I probably followed up my statement with, "for chronic migraine." Apparently I was afraid I'd be perceived as someone addicted to painful cosmetic treatments.

Non-Pharmaceutical Remedies

I'm grateful to have also found a number of therapies that don't involve medication.

Peppermint oil. It seems people have been using peppermint for years for migraine relief, and I was late to the peppermint party. I'm wary of anything with a fragrance because of my chemical "scent-sitivity." Perfume, strong laundry detergent, scented candles, air fresheners, and fragranced bath products can all have a negative effect on me and my noggin. When the essential oils fad started, I had a guard up about it. My late father-in-law had environmental allergies, and fragrances had a profound effect on his ability to breathe. We agreed that these were undoubtedly UN-essential oils.

That is, until I discovered peppermint oil. The form I use comes in a roll-on applicator. This hasn't worked to eliminate full-blown headaches, but I remember using it once at the onset of pain and was able to continue with my evening plans.

Cefaly. The most important non-pharmaceutical intervention I want to discuss is the Cefaly device. This marvelous little invention works by sending electrical impulses along the trigeminal nerve, which plays a role in migraine pain. I tell people that it's like a TENS machine for that nerve.

To use the Cefaly, the patient places a reusable electrode on their forehead, forming a "unibrow" with their eyebrows. Then the Cefaly device is attached by matching the magnets on it with those on the electrode. The user taps the Cefaly unit once for a sixty-minute acute session, or twice for a twenty-minute prevent session. It's wise to start slowly, hopefully at a time when you don't have a migraine. Until you've built up a tolerance to the strange sensation, I would advise only completing a fraction of each session. It's possible to react with a migraine if you begin using the Cefaly device too aggressively or if you start off in pain.

My first few sessions didn't go well, but I'm glad I persevered because the results have been phenomenal. I use the prevent mode daily before bed, unless *brain pain* dictates that I should opt for an acute session. It also seems to have a somewhat sedating effect, which is welcome, given it's the last item in my bedtime routine.

I have found that with the combination of Botox and Cefaly, my triptan usage has been drastically reduced. It's definitely not a cure, but it has been the closest thing I've found to a miracle in treating my headaches. If you're interested, I encourage you to read more at www.cefaly.com.

Unfortunately, all the medications and non-pharmaceutical remedies are sometimes no match for a doozy of a headache. Our family attended a beautiful outdoor summer wedding that saw Claire in the role of bridesmaid for the first time. The day presented me with many challenges. Walking around the uneven grounds of the wedding venue was tiring, and the clear and sunny day was a strain on my photosensitivity. I was out of my usual routine, and other unknown triggers may have been at play as well.

By the time the reception started, I had severe *brain pain* despite taking a triptan. As the bride was a close friend of Claire, this was an important wedding for our family; I was determined to stay as long as I could.

After dinner, we had a beautiful family picture taken. Looking at the photo, no one would guess that I was at a level nine (out of ten) on the pain scale. My *brain pain* was severe, but I was able to pose with Kevin and Claire with a convincing smile. Before all the speeches were given, my endurance for the day was completely tapped. I'd spent the day being invisibly ill, and it was time for me to disappear.

Once at home and in bed, I surrendered to the relief of the much-needed quiet and dark room.

Triggering

My headaches are triggered by a number of circumstances.

Routine. Caffeine is an interesting one because it can be a trigger but can also work to combat acute migraine pain. I alluded to the nuances of caffeine and headaches in my discussion on my headache cocktail. You've likely heard of people missing their coffee one day and having a terrible headache. Caffeine withdrawal can be a significant trigger. Any change from my usual caffeine consumption causes trouble. When I had caffeinated tea every day at breakfast, I had to make sure my tea routine didn't get interrupted. Eventually, it made sense to give up caffeinated tea altogether through a slow and careful weaning process.

Now that my caffeine baseline is essentially zero, I can use caffeine to my advantage on rare occasions. At times, I may choose to medicate with caffeine through an over-the-counter intervention containing acetaminophen and caffeine. Caffeine enhances the effectiveness of an analgesic—at least it does for *brain pain*. I try to avoid continually treating a recurring headache the same way because of the possibility of getting into a vicious cycle of withdrawal and dependency. It's important to treat a headache at the onset, intervening before it escalates. When a headache goes on for days and medication is continuously used, medication-overuse headaches become a concern.

In a similar way to a disruption in a caffeine routine, disruption in sleeping patterns can cause headaches. Many people have noted weekend headaches because they get up early for work all week and sleep in on the weekends. Unfortunately, indulging in a well-deserved lazy Saturday morning may not be in everyone's best interest.

Fermented foods. After many years of drinking water kefir, I took a holiday from it based on something I read online about fermented foods being a possible migraine trigger. Unbelievably, it seemed to make an immediate positive difference. I asked my headache neurologist if he had heard of such claims, and he confirmed that fermented foods can be triggers for some. My little experiment with stopping kefir-consumption was far from a rigorous, scientific, controlled study, but I'm interested to see if the positive trend continues. You can read more about why I began drinking water kefir in chapter eight.

Climate change. Fluctuations in weather can also pose a problem. Storms, quick changes in barometric pressure, or other variations in weather patterns often cause me *brain pain*. When I sense a headache may be thanks to a shift in the weather, I'll sometimes text friends who also experience weather-related migraines to see how they're faring. Often, many of us are in the same overcrowded migraine boat.

Seeing rosy. Eye strain is another big issue for me. I have pink-tinted glasses that I wear when in places with fluorescent or harsh LED lights. It seems to cut the glare and reduces strain. I learned about this tactic from a friend who suffered a concussion and had migraines as a result.

Virtually painful. All the video chatting we did during the pandemic was a challenge for me. I discovered that on most of these calls, the lighting would be vastly different from one participant to the next. Most people set themselves up for the chat, accommodating what would work best for them without considering how their setup will impact others. When participating in such a situation, I was often looking at bright backgrounds, frequently with lights or windows directly behind a participant. For a while, I moved my piano lessons to this format but found I ended up with a headache after each virtual lesson.

In some screen environments, I can select dark mode. I've enabled this on my devices, and when working at my computer, I use the night mode setting for my monitor. It gives the screen an orange hue that you can adjust the strength of. The goal of this setting is similar to that of blue light glasses people use when working on screens. I find it much easier to view white text on a black background over the traditional presentation of black text on a white background. With anything that is backlit, the amount of light I am staring at is greatly reduced with the dark mode scenario.

Spectacles. I used to wear glasses, but in the last twenty years, any time I wore them, I got a headache. Within a month of turning forty, I noticed difficulty focusing on what I was reading and began using reading glasses. These gave me headaches too, and I eventually embraced the wonder of multifocal contact lenses. I learned that this change in our vision as we age is called presbyopia. I dare you to find out what the Greek roots of this word are. The Greeks do not mince words.

My vision has continued to change as I add more trips around the sun to my celestial passport. I found myself struggling to continue to feel content with the prescription of my multifocal contact lenses. My optometrist worked with me to tweak the prescription, but it became evident that although this type of lens can be wonderful and was effective for me for years, its limitations were becoming apparent. More precision is available when progressive lenses are made for glasses. I took a giant leap of faith and made a significant financial investment in a pair of glasses with progressive lenses. I was terrified of the headaches that I felt were sure to ensue. I prayed about this and asked others to as well, and I'm pleased to report I have had success with my glasses! During the first week with them, I think I could hold my glasses responsible for two headaches. But then again, they could easily have been as a consequence of any of my other triggers.

My glasses came with a magnetic clip with polarized sunglass lenses. I was able to order a second clip with pink lenses like the ones I'd been using previously. It was actually a good test to see (pardon the pun) if the pink lenses were really making a difference. I was without pink lenses for a few weeks while they sorted out how to make another clip with them. I found they indeed made a big difference. Plus, my good friend Jan says I look really cool with them. She is indeed a good friend.

I relied heavily on family, Jan, and other close friends in 2002 when I received news that would change my life forever.

ONE: BRAIN PAIN

Takeaways

When you or someone you care for has headaches:
- Take children seriously. Always get advice from a trusted healthcare professional about appropriate medication use for your child.
- Anyone, including children, can benefit from rest in a quiet environment without bright lights. A cool cloth on their forehead can offer non-pharmaceutical relief.
- Keep a food and activity journal to help you determine headache triggers for you or your child.
- Be on the alert for changes in diet, routine, and weather and look for trends in their effects.
- Research medications and ask about side effects. I have found pharmacists to be a wealth of knowledge.
- Check with a doctor or pharmacist before taking medications in combination.
- If you receive massages, you may want to ask your therapist to use strokes that move away from your head.
- Stretch to keep muscles relaxed. Get advice on proper stretching from a professional, such as a physiotherapist.
- If possible, find a doctor who will probe and refer and not just prescribe.
- Stay active as you are able.
- Remember that most medications will have the greatest efficacy if taken at the onset of symptoms.
- Try non-pharmaceutical remedies. Have many tools in your headache toolbox.
- Eliminate caffeine if you can, but make sure to wean yourself slowly.

To show consideration to others who may be prone to headaches:
- Refrain from wearing fragrances. Due to olfactory fatigue, you may not realize a fragrance is lingering on clothes you wore previously.
- Offer fragrance-free soap at your place of business.
- Be mindful of volume.
- Harsh lighting can be painful for many headache sufferers. Dimmer switches and the softer and warmer LED colour temperatures can make a big difference.

- If attending a virtual video meeting, consider how you and you room will appear to others. Make sure you are the brightest part of what is seen on others' screens, with no bright lights facing the viewers.

Two
THE BIG DIAGNOSIS

Did you survive the *brain pain* chapter? There's a twist that ties into my MS story. The relevant piece is the MRI I underwent in June 2001. The last you heard, the neurologist commented on the MRI by telling me everything was normal. What I didn't mention in the previous chapter was the presence of some symptoms unrelated to head pain.

In June 2001, I was wrapping up a year as the grade 7 homeroom teacher to nineteen boys and four girls. Probably gone unnoticed by my class, I had begun stuttering and slurring my words on occasion. I say this was probably unnoticed because I noted these speech concerns most often when dealing with what professional educators refer to as *shenanigans*. On a school bus and feeling frazzled on a field trip, I gave a clear and commanding instruction to students to "S-s-si-si-sit down at once!" I also had minor dizzy spells lasting seconds at a time. I mentioned these to the neurologist, who probably concluded I was a young, stressed-out teacher, and it was June. However, in retrospect, I wonder if these symptoms were somehow related to the diagnosis you'll hear about later in this chapter. Since they didn't recur, they didn't come up with any of the other neurologists I've seen.

"We're not Alone"
The summer couldn't have been more welcome, especially because Kevin and I had decided it was the right time to add Baby Olfert to our family. Being the optimistic person I am, I assumed this would happen quickly. I was expecting to be expecting early in summer and to welcome a child the following spring. My biology does a poor job when it comes to taking orders from me, and I didn't exult in the joy of a positive pregnancy test until early the next year.

I called the beautiful Dr. Bev and described my symptoms. She offered that I could leave a urine sample at a nearby lab, and she would leave instructions for them to process the test "STAT." What a gift to have a friend and mentor as my family doctor!

I was so relieved to not have to buy another pregnancy test at the grocery store and possibly bump into someone I knew. After work, I drove to the lab STAT and left the required sample. Soon after I arrived home, Dr. Bev called to tell me there was good news.

When Kevin came home, I met him at our back entrance and simply said, "We're not alone." His gorgeous face revealed that the message was received loud and clear. On Friday, January 18, 2002, our lives changed forever.

Sleeping Leg

Earlier in the week, my left leg had fallen asleep. I experienced a pins-and-needles sensation, lasting for days. The symptom was there when I talked to Dr. Bev about what I suspected were pregnancy symptoms, so I mentioned my concerns about my leg too. When she called to let me know I was pregnant, she also emphasized the need for me to see a neurologist. I really didn't see the urgency and brushed off her concern and the symptom.

A busy evening followed with a couple of appointments, supper, and a visit with Big Sister and her husband, Duane (affectionately nicknamed Brother by Little Sister and me when we welcomed him to the family), their nine-month-old daughter, and my parents. It was especially exciting sharing the news with all of them, as it was my mom's birthday, and that's by far the best birthday present I've ever given her. Little Sister was noticeably absent. She was in her last year of her education degree and also at the beginning stages of a relationship with the man she would marry seven months later. Our family is close, and she was informed by phone call as soon as possible.

Naïve

I casually mentioned the sleeping leg fiasco, which piqued the interest of Big Sister and Brother, who both work in the medical field. They encouraged me to see the neurologist sooner rather than later. I was still in the dark as to why two doctors and a nurse were so keen to have me see a nervous system specialist. Being naïve comes in handy when all you really want to do is be excited about a new pregnancy.

In my innocence, I also mentioned to my grade 7 class the funny feeling I had in my left leg. My students and I had a fun rapport, and I often told them about personal goings-on, especially when they involved such trivial and benign antics as limbs falling asleep.

Three days after the positive pregnancy test, I was informed that I had an appointment in two days to see the neurologist. It was an inconvenient time, and I wasn't sure I could get time off work. I'm quite sure I tried to reschedule. When I spoke to Dr. Bev later in the day, she informed me kindly that specialist appointments are not to be dealt with so flippantly, and I should go out of my way to keep the appointment. Subsequently, I had an important call with the principal of my school. It went something like this:

Me:	Hi, John. I need to tell you something. Okay. I'm pregnant. I'm sorry.
Principal:	Congratulations!
Me:	It's just that I know it means you'll have to hire someone else for my mat leave, and I just feel so bad for inconveniencing you. And another thing. I've been having some weird sensations with a numb leg. My doctor really thinks I need to see a neurologist, and I was wondering if I could get Wednesday afternoon off to do that.
Principal:	Of course. You need to look after your health. I will take care of a substitute for you.

Neurology
It's time to rip off the bandage.

When I went into the neurologist's office for my appointment, the receptionist was exceptionally nice to me and seemed somewhat apologetic. As I went into the room with the physician, I may have even sensed some sympathetic and pleading eyes following me from behind the front desk.

I briefly described to the neurologist what had been going on for the last week, and then he apologized, which made sense of the receptionist's odd behaviour. He told me he was very sorry, and that although he'd told me last summer that my MRI was normal, it actually showed some abnormalities—two to be precise—in the form of white spots on my brain. This pair of lesions and my clinical symptoms were consistent with multiple sclerosis (MS). He explained that he couldn't formally diagnose me without a follow-up MRI, but that would have to wait until after my pregnancy.

Are you mad? This is when people usually get upset. How did this even happen? How does a neurology office get white spots on the brain wrong? The explanation I was given went something like this: *Somehow your abnormal MRI results were put in the pile of normal ones and were reported to you incorrectly as a result.* At least that's what I have convinced myself I was told. Brother suggested another theory a couple of decades later: people with nothing amiss neurologically can have lesions show up on an MRI of the brain. At the time of the MRI, I didn't present clinically with MS symptoms, so the white spots on the MRI may not have been viewed as a remarkable finding.

Telling Husband
Now I had something to tell my dear husband that was nothing like the happy news I'd shared with him less than a week before. I drove home from the neurologist's office with exceptionally wet cheeks and did the most rational thing I could. I called my person while he was at work, crying my face off and saying, "Kevin, I might have MS!" The poor man—having his day interrupted, receiving potentially life-altering news, comforting his wife, and being expected to complete his work day productively.

Being an Open Book Can Be Risky
When I returned to school the next day, I had a different outlook on being so transparent with my students. Knowing a numb leg could be a sign of trouble with my nervous system, I wished I hadn't shared those details with the class. As if on cue, one of the boys in my class blurted out something like, "Mrs. O, did you know a numb leg could mean you have MS? My mom told me." I too often forgot that what a teacher shares in the classroom is frequently passed on to parents, and both students and their parents can become curious about the teacher's life.

My symptoms were invisible to those around me, and I wish I hadn't drawn attention by sharing about the odd sensations I was experiencing.

Anticipation Versus Ongoing Symptoms
After a little while, I settled into being excited about being pregnant and put the possibility of MS to the back of my mind. I had something amazing to focus my mental energy on and chose to do that. However, two more times before the end of my second trimester, I had a recurrence of the symptoms in my left leg. My third trimester was free of nervous system distractions, which was most welcome, as there was plenty of nesting I needed to tend to much more urgently.

> *I had something amazing to focus my mental energy on and chose to do that.*

Eleven days after our due date, we joyfully welcomed our Claire Bear.

Official

About two-and-a-half months after Claire's birth, new symptoms developed, and I found these troubling. My left hip and leg became weak, and I began to walk with a bit of a limp. Dr. Bev sent me straight back to the same neurologist I'd seen previously. I got in to see him quickly, and he said that even without a second MRI, he felt confident in making a diagnosis. After almost twelve months of living under a question mark, I was officially told I had relapsing remitting multiple sclerosis. The last words I ever heard from the man who diagnosed me were "Have a good life" as I walked out of his office with a fistful of pamphlets. Those words hit me hard and made me wonder if I wasn't supposed to have a good life or if good lives aren't offered to people with MS. As it turns out, I've been given many years to write the book on whether those thoughts were valid. Spoiler alert: I have an *exceptionally* good life.

No Regrets

Here's why I don't need anyone to be mad about the thought-to-be misfiled MRI results:

What if we'd thought I might have MS in the summer of 2001? Would we have pursued more testing? Would I have started treatment for MS? Would there be a Claire? We can absolutely *not* imagine our lives without her and wouldn't change anything in this story.

I never did speak to Mr. Dr. "Have a Good Life" again because he referred me to the MS clinic, where I was placed under the care of Dr. Maria Melanson, an MS neurologist. Getting this diagnosis forced me onto a steep learning curve as I digested a plethora of information about what happens when the nervous system doesn't function as God designed.

Takeaways

- Filter what you say and how much you share depending on your audience. It's good to share our lives with others, but not all information is meant for all ears.
- Take specialist appointments seriously.
- Sometimes in life we receive life-altering news. Acknowledge your emotions and allow yourself to cry. Eventually you'll need to face life with a new perspective and figure out how to live well in a new reality. But don't rush through the initial shock and grief.
- Avoid perseverating on events you have no control over and can't change. We don't see the big picture, and there is so much to be hopeful for. We can't change the past and often have no control over our circumstances, but we can always work on our future. That might mean choosing to be proactive and taking steps that will pay off long-term. We live our lives one day at a time and can choose to have eyes that look for blessings.

Three
MS SCHOOL

One thing I've learned from over two decades of living with multiple sclerosis is to not assume that basic facts about MS are common knowledge. What follows are some MS basics that I've learned over more than twenty years of living with it. It would be impossible to provide footnotes, as this information has come to me slowly over time. It's also possible that there have been more recent developments, so please do your own responsible research involving knowledgeable healthcare professionals before making any decisions or assumptions about your health.

MS Varieties
When I was diagnosed with MS, I read about the following three forms of the disease:

1. Relapsing remitting MS (RRMS). Since this best describes my situation, most of my comments about MS in this book will relate to relapsing remitting multiple sclerosis. This presentation is characterized by relapses (also known as attacks or exacerbations) followed by periods of remission.
2. Secondary progressive MS (SPMS). Relapsing remitting MS often eventually transitions to the secondary progressive phase of the disease, where there is more progression and fewer relapses. Secondary refers to it being a secondary presentation of MS. It's impossible to start that way; relapsing remitting MS always precedes it.
3. Primary progressive MS (PPMS). The word *primary* here indicates that this form of MS didn't originate as another type. In other words, primary progressive MS doesn't start out as relapsing remitting MS, as secondary progressive MS does. This progressive form is characterized by increasing progression from the beginning. It's rarer than the first two varieties mentioned.
4. If you're searching online for the different types of MS, you will likely only find the above three referenced. However, there is a fourth worth

mentioning. Within about five years of my diagnosis, a friend of mine also heard the news that MS would be part of her story. Her disease presentation differed from mine, and it took longer for a clear diagnosis. For a while, I thought she had primary progressive MS until one day she explained to me that hers was actually progressive relapsing MS (PRMS). I understand from her that it's the rarest form, affecting only 5 per cent of MS patients. As its name suggests, this kind has both progression and relapses. When I asked my neurologist to weigh in, he confirmed that progressive relapsing MS is indeed an MS presentation and it's sometimes called active progressive MS.

Sometime after I was diagnosed, I heard the term *clinically isolated syndrome* (CIS). This describes a single episode of neurological symptoms. CIS can, but doesn't always, develop into MS.

Undiscriminating
MS patients include members of both sexes. Men tend to be hit harder with primary progressive MS and therefore experience more progression than women. However, MS is more prevalent overall in women than in men.

Autoimmune
An autoimmune disease is one in which a person's immune system attacks a healthy part of the body. In my case, my immune system is attacking my nervous system—specifically the myelin sheath around my nerves. I imagine it as a civil war going on in my body. Autoimmune diseases are lopsided battles, as the immune system lashes out on defenceless cells. My nervous system is taking my Mennonite roots a little too far and is practising pacifism in epic proportions.

There are many autoimmune diseases, and you probably know more people with one than you realize. Among my friends and family are people living with Addison's disease, celiac disease, Crohn's disease, Graves' disease, lupus, various presentations of multiple sclerosis, psoriasis, and type I diabetes.

All about the CNS
When Mommy texts about CNS, she's usually referring to the <u>c</u>hicken <u>n</u>oodle <u>s</u>oup she wants to bring to someone feeling under the weather. In a slightly more common use of CNS, the <u>c</u>entral <u>n</u>ervous <u>s</u>ystem is being referenced. The central nervous system comprises the brain and spinal cord. Through Magnetic Resonance Imaging (MRI), lesions or plaques can be observed as "white spots" on the brains and spinal cords of MS patients. They indicate areas of damage

in the central nervous system. Nerves are part of the nervous system but not considered part of the *central* nervous system.

High Decibel Warning

I dare you to do an Internet search for "MRI sounds." When I first had MRIs in the early 2000s, the noises from the machines were lower in pitch than they are now and often sounded a bit like a jackhammer. Brother could mimic these sounds with astounding precision. I've always been given ear protection when having an MRI, and at first, I'd often fall asleep during the scans. Lately, the noises have been higher in pitch and have more of a digital feel to them. I find them rather annoying because they're harder to block out, and with the lower jackhammer sounds, I used to be able to enjoy a forty-five-minute nap in those tubes.

No Metal Aloud?

MRIs are a common part of an MS diagnosis. They're also used throughout a person's disease course to give doctors more information about the stability of MS in their patient. There's an intentional misspelling in the above section heading for three reasons:

1. MRI machines definitely express themselves "aloud"—very loudly indeed.
2. I *mis*spelled *allowed* as *aloud* because there are *mis*conceptions about MRIs. I also can't resist a play on words and a punny joke.
3. I am fortunate to know an MRI technologist, who was able to enlighten me and clear up some of my *mis*understandings, even though I have more than two dozen MRIs under my belt (although not literally under my belt, because belt-wearing isn't permitted during the procedure).

An important screening process is in place before you're scanned to ensure a safe and successful MRI. Magnetic Resonance Imaging uses massive and incredibly strong magnets. It's important to be careful around such a powerful force and to understand what is safe and what is risky.

The first part of the screening is a paper questionnaire asking about metallic items you might have in your body or on your person. You need to answer yes or no for each item, and it can feel somewhat tedious—especially for someone who has quite a lot of experience receiving MRIs. Once in a while, though, I've spotted an item that I hadn't seen on the list previously. Leggings from a particular store come to mind, and I felt baffled by that one.

The second stage is an interview with an MRI technologist who has reviewed your answers and also asks further questions—sometimes just for clarification.

I asked about the leggings at this point in the screening, and it was explained to me that the particular brand in question routinely incorporates metal fibres into their clothes.

The technologist and survey pose a lot of questions, and this may lead you to conclude that no metal is allowed in an MRI. This is a common misconception. Metals that respond to a magnet and are said to have ferromagnetism are of concern. Cheaper metal jewellery may contain nickel, which could be an issue, but high-quality metal is usually used in most piercings. People with tattoos are imaged all the time with no issue, although the questionnaire does ask if you have tattoos. For years I thought that meant a tattooed body wouldn't be scan-able. Finding out this is only true in rare cases has not prompted me to acquire some ink of my own. At one scan, the technologist noticed I was wearing copper-sole socks, which she asked me to remove before we proceeded with the MRI. We were in the MRI room when I took them off, and I asked if I should move them to the locker assigned to me earlier. I was imagining them flying into the machine and attacking me. It wasn't an issue, but metal-containing clothing could heat up somewhat, and that would be uncomfortable. Ultimately, the screening process is important to ensure a harmless and comfortable procedure.

The main culprits for concern and the only absolute contraindications for MRI are electronic devices and metallic implants that aren't firmly implanted. Examples include pacemakers, spinal stimulators, some aneurysm clips, and metal in the eye. However, the vast majority of metal used in surgical implants is not ferromagnetic, which means it doesn't respond to a magnet at all. This includes titanium, platinum, and aluminum; there is no need to worry if you've had a joint replaced or have spinal hardware.

Safety is paramount, but another consideration is the quality of the images. Clear pictures will be the most beneficial to doctors and their patients. In my mid-thirties, I had the pleasure of wearing a full set of orthodontic metal braces for about eighteen months. Anyone who knows me well will understand the extreme sarcasm in that sentence—the process of having my teeth aligned was not a pleasure. As I usually have an MRI annually, sure enough, Mrs. Middle-Aged Metal Mouth found herself scheduled for an MRI. I assumed my oral hardware would be a major contraindication, especially for a brain scan. However, I was told that the metal in the braces would be just fine in the scanner. I still found it hard to believe and was probably a little more grateful than usual for the bulb in my hand that I could squeeze in case of emergency. I remember imagining the terror of the braces ripping off my teeth and flying toward the massive magnet. I didn't feel any panic once the MRI was underway, because everything felt normal. However, the scans were almost completely useless. I needed to have new imaging done after my braces were removed.

Unlike with braces, there *is* a major concern about loose metal objects in people's pockets. Pocket knives and loose coins should not enter the scan room when a procedure is underway. They may escape the person's clothing and fly across the room because they're unrestrained; if they did make a sudden exit, they could cause impalement.

Something you may want to know for your convenience is that if you are unfortunate enough to enter the scanner room with your phone or wallet, the electronics might be wrecked or the magnetic stripe on your credit cards could get wiped out.

Messed up Myelin

In a similar way to insulation that encases wires, our nerves are covered in a myelin sheath. If a wire isn't protected by insulation, electrical messages aren't transmitted properly. If the myelin sheath around a nerve is damaged, messages sent by the brain are slowed down or interrupted. For example, due to damaged myelin blocking a message from my brain, one of my quadriceps may not realize that my brain is asking it to flex. The result might be weakness in my leg. When I experience a sensation like burning or numbness, I wonder what message is being interrupted.

Passing It On

MS is 100 per cent not contagious; there is no risk of catching it from someone else, but there may be a hereditary component at work sometimes. Soon after I was diagnosed, an MS nurse told me about this faint association. She explained that MS has a weak genetic link, and I continue to hold on to that. We don't spend any time or energy worrying about Claire getting MS. There are cases of a parent and child both having MS, but this is not the norm. The only advice we've been given with respect to Claire is for her to take Vitamin D daily, which is a recommendation our family doctor would give anyway.

> *MS is 100 per cent not contagious; there is no risk of catching it from someone else, but there may be a hereditary component at work sometimes.*

High Latitude

MS tends to be more prevalent in places farther from the equator, and I've heard it spoken of as a *high latitude disease*. Theories abound about a link to Vitamin D, and I take four thousand international units daily on the advice of my MS clinic. The Vitamin D isn't intended to be a curative agent, but supplementation is helpful for my general health. Thanks to being sensitive to both light and heat, I spend less time in the sun getting Vitamin D naturally than most people.

Interestingly, the neurologist I started seeing in 2023 is from Lebanon. He explained to Kevin and me that Lebanon has a disproportionately higher incidence of MS than other lower latitude countries. It's thought that there's a link to Lebanese people having trouble converting Vitamin D.

Sensitivity to Heat

Heat can be an enemy of MS patients. It exhausts me and can aggravate symptoms. I've heard of people with MS who actually do better in warmer climates and will spend time in places like Mexico. On purpose. This baffles me, because my experience with heat is drastically different. In fact, after having a warm shower, my foot drop may be worse, and I might be more fatigued than usual for up to an hour or more. This is called a pseudo-relapse because it's "fake news." There is no new disease activity, just an exacerbation of symptoms mimicking a relapse. The same phenomenon can occur in the presence of an infection, which I will discuss further in the next chapter. When the heat or infection is no longer present, given time or treatment, the symptoms begin to abate.

Treatments

I started my first disease-modifying therapy (DMT) shortly after seeing my first MS specialist. I am now on my fourth such therapy. The options for DMTs were limited when I was diagnosed in the early 2000s; I remember hearing about four injectable medications. The list has grown immensely since then and includes subcutaneous (below the skin, into fat) injections, intramuscular (into muscle) injections, infusions (given intravenously), and pills taken orally.

More Than Just R and R

Relapsing remitting multiple sclerosis has manifested itself in a few ways, at least for me.

Relapses and remissions. Relapses occur out of the blue and can last from days to months. They can be sensory or motor. Motor relapses affect muscle strength. I was surprised to learn that vision relapses are classified as motor relapses; they involve the muscles of the eyes. I suppose I never thought about eyes in that way. When we think about muscles, biceps are more likely to come to mind. Maybe the eye muscles are called "eye-ceps."

For a motor relapse, a large burst of prednisone given orally or intravenously can speed up recovery. The usual dose for me has been 1,000 mg once per day for three or five days. Treating with steroids in this way won't alter the ultimate outcome of the relapse, but the treatment will often shorten the duration of it.

A period of remission is the flipside to a relapse. When a relapse is over, the patient will often return to their baseline.

Symptoms. Another aspect of relapsing remitting MS is the presence of symptoms, which are often experienced daily. For me, these have included fatigue, trouble with balance, sensitivity to heat, various issues with elimination, nerve pain, and muscle spasms. There are medications to relieve some of the impact of these symptoms, as well as strategies learned in physical and occupational therapy.

Relapses and remissions made sense to me because they're in the name of this type of MS. The symptoms component threw me for a loop. I thought getting relapses was more than enough; I wasn't prepared to deal with daily symptoms as well. Honestly, I wasn't prepared to manage anything MS imposed on me. How does one get ready for the surprise arrival of a chronic illness?

Fatigue presented itself as a symptom early in my disease course. Within six months of diagnosis, I was also living with nerve pain. You may have heard about nerve pain, also called neuropathic pain, in relation to shingles, diabetes, cancer, and other conditions. The nerve pain I experience is usually only in my legs. It's more uncomfortable than painful most of the time, and it feels somewhat as if my legs are restless yet different (it isn't restless leg syndrome). It's most noticeable at night and can keep me from sleeping.

Chronic symptoms. There's a difference between a symptom and a chronic symptom, even though both might be experienced chronically. I can't imagine you'll trust anything I say anymore. I promise you—I am not making this up.

I first heard about chronic symptoms when I informed my MS neurologist that I had a patch of skin on my left shoulder blade that always felt as though it were burning and itchy. Dr. Marriott explained to me that my body was remembering a former relapse. Apparently, I had previously experienced a sensory relapse with those symptoms, and now I seem to be recalling those good old days and replaying them constantly. I've given my burning patch of skin a proper name and refer to it as Itchy Spot. I will sometimes ask Kevin or Claire to scratch Itchy Spot, never "the itchy spot." This uninvited friend is a constant irritation and invisible to others but annoyingly perceptible by me. In contrast, my other chronic symptom, foot drop, is not an invisible one, as it has slowed my walking and added a slight limp along with a fashionable brace.

Many times I've asked the nurses and doctors at the MS clinic if my disease course has shifted into the secondary progressive MS phase, and I've always been told that it's still classified as relapsing remitting MS. Often I've interpreted chronic symptoms as progression. However, based on my clinical history, I'm still living the relapsing remitting dream. Even if I had transitioned to secondary progressive MS, my treatments would remain as they are now.

It's a Canadian Thing, Eh?

Canada has one of the highest rates of MS globally. The Prairie provinces (Alberta, Saskatchewan, and Manitoba) appear to be a hotbed of MS in Canada, and that's exactly where I happen to live. I haven't heard any sound theories on why MS occurs much more often in these provinces than elsewhere in Canada.

As I quickly found out, *learning about* MS is drastically different from *living with* the disease. And the process of learning from experiencing MS first-hand was often a bumpy one.

Takeaways

- Do research on your health conditions and use trusted sources. It's better to rely on knowledge from professionals than to consult Dr. Google.
- Just as it's important to take specialist appointments seriously, completing diagnostic tests your doctor has ordered is also imperative. If you have questions, ask your doctor or the technologist performing the procedure. Always ask questions rather than jumping to conclusions.
- Refrain from doling out advice on others' situations unless you have listened to understand first and are actually an authority on the matter. Assume that they have done extensive research and spoken to many professionals. Telling people what they *should* do is judgemental, but offering what they *could* do honours their right to choose. When I get "should advice," my internal response to such "help" can be summed up in a meme I once saw on social media: "Thanks for the advice, but what I really need are minions." Sick people will usually love minions disguised as window-washers or gourmet chefs.

Four
NOT MY FAVOURITE ROLLERCOASTER

Our family took a trip to Florida when I was in grade 6. One of the highlights was going to Busch Gardens, where they had two rollercoasters with upside down loops. Big Sister and Dad were keen to experience these thrills, but I was hesitant. Actually, I was adamant about my desire to stay on the ground close to Little Sister and Mom. However, Dad reasoned that given a little encouragement, I would change my tune. Alas, it came to pass that I found myself head over heels on the Scorpion and the Python.

Quick aside: For a long time I have thought the phrase "head over heels" made no sense. Whenever we say "head over heels," we're talking about a situation where heels are actually over head, not the other way around. Or we're in love, and that's a state beyond explanation. English idioms can be ridiculous.

There I was, *heels over head,* and absolutely loving it! It turns out Daddy was right after all—not that I would have easily admitted it to him at the time.

Relapsing remitting MS often feels like a rollercoaster with all the ups and downs, although it would be more accurate to talk about the "somewhat normals" and "downs." MS is not a coaster anyone encouraged me to try out, and it's not one I would have asked to go on. Screaming is not an approach I have adopted to distract myself from the scary parts, though. I doubt screaming would help with MS; it would be hard to do so long enough to create the desired distraction.

Disease-Modifying Therapies (DMTs)

I was diagnosed in December 2002 and was referred to Dr. Maria Melanson at my local MS clinic. My first appointment with Dr. Melanson was early in 2003. She was eager to get me started on a disease-modifying therapy as soon as possible. The one complication was that I was still nursing Claire. It was emotional to have to wean my infant at four months, because it was earlier than I'd wanted to, and I was also saddened over the reason why I had to stop. I quickly learned about DMTs called *interferons.* Dr. Melanson recommended I start on an interferon called *Rebif*. I wasn't thrilled to learn I'd be administering injections, but I wasn't trembling in fear at the prospect either.

Rebif

My life has been blessed beyond measure by Big Sister. Aside from being an amazing sibling over the years, she's an incredible nurse. Soon after my MS diagnosis, she shared with Mom, "Maybe I became a nurse so I could take care of Robyn." Mom told me about their conversation a number of years later. It hasn't been so dramatic to cause me to need twenty-four-hour home care from Big Sister, but she has been tremendously helpful and compassionate toward me in a way her chosen career makes especially meaningful.

Long before she made that comment to Mom, she was already the best big sister anyone could hope for. From the blustery Winnipeg morning when she trudged through the snow just ahead of me on our trek to elementary school, telling me to just look down and walk in her footprints, to paving the way in an intimidating junior high school, I always appreciated the guided tours she gave me.

Little did we know a very different guided tour than that awaited us. Big Sister came with me to my training session for the Rebif injections. Having her support made a hard appointment less nerve-wracking. It felt good to have my own medical person along and reassuring to know I had someone to help me out if I forgot any of the details in the process. She's also wonderful when it comes to asking the right technical health questions, and her presence gave me assurance and confidence.

The nurse trained us with the Rebif auto injector, which worked similarly to an EpiPen. I could choose sites from areas on my abdomen, upper legs, and hip-buttock area. For the first needle, I opted for the abdomen so that I wouldn't need to undress to access the site. I don't remember much about the appointment, but I can recall as if it were yesterday the moment I first sensed the drug enter my body.

The instant the medicine went in, I broke down in tears. Big Sister and the training nurse were immediately concerned and started asking me questions, assuming the injection had been extremely painful. But the tears were simply a release, acknowledging how overwhelming everything had become. The second that Rebif was released in me was precisely when MS became real to me. Yes, there was some physical discomfort with the injection, but the tears were a response to the culmination of an abundance of emotions.

Soon, administering Rebif every Monday, Wednesday, and Friday became routine. Claire hasn't known her mom without MS, and seeing me give myself needles was never alarming for her. In fact, we intentionally included her in the process, as we sought to normalize something often seen as frightening to children. Eventually we invited Claire to press the button on the injector to trigger the release of the needle. She proudly told others, "I gave Mommy a needle!" She saw me get needles so often that she would frequently remark how much I *loved* needles. Her interpretation was not accurate, though; I did not *love* needles, but I chose to have a brave attitude toward them. I explained to her that my "liking needles" was about appreciating the help they gave me and not enjoying the feeling of them.

Claire has grown into an amazing, compassionate adult who is unfazed by differences or disabilities. She's planning a career in occupational therapy, where these traits will be a phenomenal asset. Although she finds getting needles uncomfortable physically and mentally, when she was twenty, she bravely donated blood for the first time. And since this is my book, I get to brag about her if I want to.

When the neurologist diagnosed me with MS, he explained various aspects of the disease, including a brief overview of the disease-modifying therapies. He mentioned that the treatments were so expensive, no one could really afford them. Before I had a chance to panic over the cost, he told me about the provincial drug program, which would cover most of the expense.

Rewards?

An unexpected perk was revealed at the Rebif training session. The nurse explained that I was welcome to have my prescriptions filled wherever I wanted to, but I would probably be happy to know of a rewards program at a certain pharmacy. Conveniently, her suggestion would have been my first choice for a pharmacy anyway, and we were already using the points program she promoted. We received our rewards based on the full cost of the drug, which included a small amount from us and a substantial contribution from the provincial drug program. Thanks to the points, we were able to get a couple of larger toys for Claire, a camcorder (which was a hot ticket item in the early 2000s), and flights for a family vacation. This perk was nice, but I would have been elated to pass up the rewards points in exchange for a clean bill of health. When life gives you lemons, sometimes the lemonade looks like toys and plane tickets.

Manual Injection Lessons

Other than the points program, we learned more about Rebif as time went on. One of our insights involved strategies to make injections more comfortable.

This involved injecting manually, which is something I would never have imagined I'd be able to do. As the training nurse informed us, I didn't *have* to use the auto injector; I could choose to manually inject Rebif.

I was curious about how the experience would differ with manual injections. Big Sister was skilled and seasoned in giving needles this way, so one day I invited her to give my injection to me in the traditional way. We watched her give the injection, and after that, Kevin and I felt confident we could do it ourselves. I learned that I prefer Rebif to be administered as slowly as possible, as the pain then became almost imperceptible. We would give the injections so slowly that it could take up to one minute to complete that phase of the process. With the auto injector, that part was over in a few painful seconds. I appreciated the way Kevin cared for me with patience and attention to detail. He is a natural caregiver, and I give him many opportunities to care for me.

Magical Drug?

So, Robyn, did it work? Did Rebif do what it was supposed to do? It's impossible to know for sure because there aren't two versions of my life to compare—Rebif life versus non-Rebif life. The disease-modifying therapies don't claim to be curative but rather aim to reduce the frequency and severity of MS attacks. It seems those goals were probably accomplished, at least to some degree. I did continue to get relapses, and some certainly impacted my day-to-day reality more than others.

The year 2003 was definitely one of learning what a rollercoaster ride relapsing remitting multiple sclerosis can be. I think back now to how often I called the MS clinic's nurses' line and feel sheepish for being somewhat dramatic about all that was happening to me. Eventually, I learned to ride the MS rollercoaster with a more even-keel outlook. I don't blame myself for reaching out frequently, though; I had been given a great deal to absorb and adapt to in a short time. It was overwhelming, especially considering I was in my postpartum days.

Pumped up on Steroids

I was thrown a curve ball when, at one point, I suddenly had a left leg motor relapse. I spoke to one of the MS nurses about it, and after she consulted Dr. Melanson, I was offered a short course of high-dose prednisone. I was completely unaware of what a normal dose of steroids was, but I understood that the 1,000 mg per day I was prescribed was a high dose. I just had no idea it was a shockingly high dose. I relayed the dosage amount to Dr. Bev, and she questioned me, saying, "You mean 100 mg?" No, I really did mean ten times that amount. The way they did high-dose steroids back in 2003 was 1,000 mg per day for three or five days followed by a taper. With the tapering schedule, the whole ordeal took about three weeks. The last time I underwent a course of high-dose prednisone was in 2014.

Before I'm ever given the green light to go on prednisone, the MS clinic insists on checking my urine for infection. *Say what now, Robyn? That seems random.* That's exactly what I thought when the MS nurse ordered a urinalysis for me. Neurology is bonkers, and I was learning about new, strange implications on a regular basis.

When an MS patient is fighting an infection like a urinary tract infection, or UTI, the inflammation can cause a pseudo-relapse—I might suddenly have profound weakness in a limb but not be having an actual relapse *But Robyn, how would you not have caught on that you had a UTI?* The answer is another new word in my vocabulary: *subclinical.* It's possible for MSers to have subclinical UTIs, meaning a patient may feel completely asymptomatic but still have an infection. *Uh, Robyn, I don't believe you. I've had a UTI, and those symptoms are obvious. There's no way you wouldn't notice.* I repeat: neurology is bonkers. I have absolutely had subclinical UTIs and have, on an embarrassing number of occasions, gone to a walk-in clinic for this reason. Often, it's discovered that I don't have a UTI, and I then feel somewhat awkward about seeking medical care for suspicion of infection. This embarrassment is unwarranted but hard not to feel. I know it's not my fault MS behaves the way it does, but I don't enjoy managing the implications of what feels like its irrational impacts. Needing to explain my situation to others can be tiring, and sometimes I just long to feel "normal." Often the response of the practitioner has a significant impact on whether I feel apologetic or embarrassed.

When at a walk-in clinic for suspicion of a UTI, the conversation usually goes something like this:

Doctor I just met:	How can I help you?
Me:	I think I have a UTI.
Doctor:	Oh, so you're having urgency and burning?
Me:	I have MS. I've had a weak leg lately and have been more tired than usual. People with MS can get subclinical UTIs, which can cause pseudo-relapses.
Doctor:	This is brand new information.
Me:	I live to educate.

The last part may be embellished slightly, but I have definitely had to explain this phenomenon to a number of general practitioners. Thankfully, my current family doctor is used to me wondering if I have a UTI and acts efficiently to deal with what's going on. And just because MS isn't already fun enough, it affects my bladder in strange ways and makes me prone to UTIs. This, in turn, makes me prone to paranoia about maybe having a bladder infection.

Taking prednisone was not exactly enjoyable. The number of large, chalky tablets I had to take was daunting with every dose. These seemed to go down best with a tall glass of chocolate milk. Side effects of prednisone included an enormous appetite, abdominal cramping, as prednisone can irritate the stomach lining, and unfamiliar energy. When I started living with MS, I began to experience profound fatigue. Being energized wasn't something I was used to!

Aside from these symptoms, I also noted mood changes. Prednisone makes everything "extra"—extra big appetite, extra wakefulness, and an extra positive outlook. Shortly into a steroids treatment, I remember having the feeling of a completely clear head with no fogginess in my thinking. I wondered, *Do people feel like this all the time? As though they're actually "with it"?* I enjoyed some of these more positive side effects, but what goes up must come down; I would crash hard after a course of steroids, especially emotionally.

There was exactly one upside to prednisone, and an upside it literally was. The amount of energy I had on prednisone was off the charts. I found it almost impossible to get any sleep and only really fell asleep at night when I took a prescription sleeping aid. The MS symptom that had affected me most was fatigue, causing me to have long nights as well as one or two naps every day. Having boundless energy was novel, and on one stint of steroids, I made Kevin a website for his part-time photography business. I wasn't a web developer by any means, but I had the time and willingness to learn, often in the middle of the night! A friend of mine who experienced a similarly large dose of steroids relayed her experience by posing the question, "Anyone need me to paint their house?"

I suppose I'm forgetting a more important upside. The prednisone ended the motor relapse early. Right. That was the actual reason for being subjected to the torture of the side effects. Prednisone has been called a miracle and a poison. I would definitely think long and hard before starting a course of steroids. I came up with a standard to help me decide whether it would be worth going through the drama again: if a motor relapse got in the way of my ability to care for myself or Claire, I would take the steroids.

Diplopia or double vision entered my vocabulary when Claire was a toddler. This was the second motor relapse I experienced for which I was given steroids intravenously. The IV approach to administering steroids is more aggressive than the oral route I was usually prescribed. By the fourth day, when I started the tapering schedule, the double vision had resolved. While experiencing double vision, I would have been unsafe to drive, and that meant depending on others to get Claire and me where we needed to go. For the three days of IV treatment, it mostly meant getting rides to the hospital for my infusion appointments. My second-last infusion was on a Saturday, and we went as a family. Kevin took a picture of Claire, which is precious to me. In the image, she's working on puzzles with me in the background in a recliner, hooked up to an IV. It was endearing to see her completely comfortable in the hospital setting, just content to be working on a puzzle close to her parents.

Young Claire story alert: When I was experiencing diplopia, one day Claire kissed me on the cheek, grabbed my face, and told me she wanted to kiss me on "the other head." I then replied, "You're the one with two heads!" It made us both laugh, and laughter was certainly welcome during those hard days.

Optic Nerve

Speaking of vision relapses, I've had optic neuritis once. It was in February 2011 and made me feel as though I were wearing dirty glasses. Optic neuritis occurs when there is damage to the optic nerve, and it's often how MS presents. I'm grateful my optic nerve has behaved itself aside from the 2011 attack. Hopefully, we're all learning not to take our optic nerves for granted.

Back to School

If you inferred I was on maternity leave when I received my diagnosis, you'd be correct. During my leave, I applied for long-term disability benefits. My request for benefits was eventually approved, but the insurance company essentially said, "We believe you when you say you're fatigued, but we think you can still work parttime." Just before Claire turned one year, I returned to classroom teaching in a jobshare scenario in a 40 per cent of full-time capacity. I loved teaching my students, but being employed, even in a scaled-back position, was too demanding. MS fatigue is one of the most common complaints of MS patients, and it's a formidable challenge to manage.

> *MS fatigue is one of the most common complaints of MS patients, and it's a formidable challenge to manage.*

I was also suffering cognitively. When there were repeated occurrences of me giving instructions to my class and starting a sentence only to forget how I meant to finish it, I knew MS was impacting my ability to educate effectively.

Do you also recall the student in my class who so helpfully pointed out that my numb leg could be a sign of MS? Yeah, so I had a bit of pride about all that. I didn't want my students, past or present, to know I had MS. As a result, mum was the word when I went back to teaching after my maternity leave. I told few people about my diagnosis until I had to, and I lived with my secret invisible diagnosis and drama.

When it was decided that I'd go on medical leave, something finally needed to be said. I told my class in tears, "I have a disease. It's called MS." I asked my ever-supportive principal, Mr. John Sawatzky, to be present while I shared with the class, explaining to him, "I know I'm going to cry when I tell them, and I just want you there to explain that the tears aren't because I'm so messed up about having MS. Rather, I'm sad to be leaving, as I have really enjoyed teaching them."

I should have taken a hint from my students. One of them had type I diabetes, and the class was definitely aware of it, as he'd gone into insulin shock at school. Another boy had cerebral palsy (CP) and walked with a noticeable limp. This student was open about his CP, and, looking back, I wonder if being more transparent about MS would have been helpful in normalizing some of what my students were going through. In fact, after I "came clean" with the class, the student with cerebral palsy seemed to offer his solace to me, comforting me as he compared my situation to his own.

People have often asked me if I miss teaching. By that, they mean *teaching in a classroom*. My last day of teaching in a classroom was the last day of school before the Christmas break. By the time the first day of school started again in January, I knew with certainty that I wouldn't miss teaching in a classroom. Being home with Claire with all the energy I could muster invested in my own child felt so much better. I had been pouring myself into teaching other people's children and feeling I only had leftover energy for my own offspring. I hear working moms *without* chronic conditions lament about the struggle of having enough energy for every aspect of their lives. It was time I gave myself a break and recognized what I was up against.

When I left on medical leave, the parents of my students reached out with generous encouragement. One parent, who was also a teacher, wrote the following words in a card to me: "Do you ever notice yourself saying, 'I teach,' not 'I am a teacher'?" I hadn't noticed, but it makes sense. I joke when I say, "I live to educate," but it has some truth. Now I enjoy my role as a piano teacher in my small private studio and am thrilled I can combine my skills in music and teaching.

SAHM (Stay-At-Home-Mom) Uses Drastic Measures

Although I wouldn't have chosen the circumstances under which it happened, I was abundantly thankful for the privilege of being a stay-at-home mom to Claire. The reality of why I was receiving long-term disability benefits sat heavily with me. In a sense, I took my daughter to work with me every day. My new job description emphasized taking care of myself, which meant napping every day. "Sleep when the baby sleeps" was an effective strategy, until Claire stopped napping. My reality changed when the napping toddler phase ended. Many times, one of Claire's grandmas would spend time with her while I rested. This made a difference in lessening the guilt I felt about the disturbing tactics to which I resorted in order to cope with my need to rest and also keep a small child safe.

I hope you're sitting down before reading the alarming disclosure that follows.

I let Claire watch a *Franklin the Turtle* video for forty-five minutes. Every. Single. Day. Small children are big fans of repetition, and this worked to my advantage. We had a selection of *Franklin* VHS tapes, which took turns playing in our VCR. Anyone who doesn't know what I'm talking about will have the tools to ask the Internet to explain. Much to my husband's disbelief, I can view the same movie more than once or even twice. I do not, however, have what it takes to enjoy the same preschool video as often as the target audience does. I felt so guilty about letting her watch a video *on a screen* every day and not constantly being engaged in actively playing with her.

I think I would be hard-pressed to find many moms who parented to the standard to which I was trying to hold myself. My mom, whom I hold on a mothering pedestal, was a stay-at-home-mom, and I remember watching thirty minutes of *Mr. Dressup* followed by sixty minutes of *Sesame Street* regularly before I was forced into formal education. I mentioned my guilt over all of this to Claire when she was in her late teens. Her jaw dropped as she said to me, "Are you kidding me? I thought that was the best!" Sometimes I wonder if upon hearing the *Franklin* theme song again, I would still be lulled to sleep. I was in survival mode. I knew I needed to rest, and lying on the couch with my daughter on a small chair beside me, watching her video, was how I accomplished this. Each video contained about five short stories. It would be a rare day when I wouldn't be asleep before the end of the first story.

Parenthood Round Two?

In 2004, Kevin and I were talking about adding a second Baby Olfert to our family. I discussed our desire for another child early in my interactions with the MS clinic. Dr. Melanson relayed the message, "We would never discourage you from having another child, but we would advise you to act on that sooner rather than later." She definitely wanted me on a disease-modifying therapy but didn't want to interfere with our personal family planning decisions. We made the choice for me to go off Rebif as well as gabapentin, which I was on for the neuropathic pain in my legs.

If I was putting too much pressure on myself to get pregnant as soon as possible the first time, this burden to get pregnant again was quickly intensified exponentially. The conversation I had with my body went something like this:

Robyn:	Okay, Body. We're on the clock. Get pregnant fast. I need to get back on Rebif.
Body:	Bwahahaha. You don't seem to know how this works. You're stressing me out. I can't work under these conditions.
Robyn:	Please?
Body:	I don't make the rules. No baby for you!

We had a hunch that Rebif was helping during the time I was on it, but during my hiatus from it, we became absolutely persuaded of the difference it had made. It didn't take long for frequent and difficult relapses to wreak havoc on my body, and our quest to expand our family came to an end within a matter of months. My reasons for crying did a 180° turn. One day I was weeping because I wasn't pregnant, and the next day I would have sobbed had I become pregnant. I was given complete peace about the decision. Although Kevin and I were unified on the choice to stop "trying," it took him longer to have similar peaceful feelings. We were at a Christmas gathering not long after we ended our family-expansion pursuits, and he found it triggering to see one of the families leave with three children in tow.

When we were pursuing pregnancy the first time, the only other person who knew about our plans was Dr. Bev. For round two, we included many people close to us, as we sought their support in friendship and prayer. One of those people was my cousin Gabe, with whom Kevin often had lunch in the middle of their work days, as they both worked downtown. When Kevin told him about our decision to stop trying, Gabe remarked, "Well, you nailed it with the first one!" We both loved the way he shared his support. We reminded ourselves of that truth regularly, and it was easy to remember. I fell in love with Claire all over again and started to value every moment with her and every memory we were making. I have a clear picture in my head of pushing her stroller on the way back from the park, heels over head in love with the little girl entrusted to our care.

Our small family of three is close, and we're all content with Claire's only-child status. When people first hear about Claire, we often get questions such as "Just the one?" and "Do you have any other children?" Sometimes it feels like there's an implied suggestion that having *just the one* child is an inferior family structure. But I know these are asked innocently and in the spirit of making conversation. How is my new acquaintance supposed to know our history and inquire accordingly? I often find myself wondering about other people's family structure too and try to pose questions carefully.

Changing Treatments

When we decided to no longer pursue adding to our family, I returned to the same treatment course I'd been on with Rebif. Unfortunately, the results weren't as promising as they'd been the first time. Dr. Melanson offered me the opportunity to participate in a clinical trial. We decided that I would do my part for science while also hoping to be part of a breakthrough; I became a lab rat, guinea pig—you pick the rodent.

The clinical trial involved getting monthly infusions and frequent MRI scans, and it ended quite anticlimactically. When it was over, Dr. Melanson suggested I try Betaseron. In December 2006, I made the switch to this disease-modifying therapy. I gave myself injections of Betaseron every other day and included Kevin and Claire in the process of mixing the medication. A bonus was how much less painful these injections were compared to the ones for Rebif. Rebif requires a preservative, as it's premixed; the preservative's pH level is much different than that of the human body, and it caused a painful burning sensation as a result.

Years later, I mentioned the clinical trial and asked if anyone knew if anything ever became of it. Apparently, it hadn't proven to be effective, and the drug being researched had ceased to be pursued.

Revolving Door of Neurologists

In March 2007, I was assigned a new neurologist, Dr. Esfahani, as Dr. Melanson was offered a position in the United States. I was sad to see her go, but I continued to receive good care from Dr. Esfahani as well as the MS nurses. I didn't have many appointments to get to know my new doctor. I generally have a neurology appointment annually, and when things are going smoothly without clinical trial participation, one visit each year is all I expect. I saw him fewer than a handful of times.

In March 2011, I had my first appointment with Dr. Marriott, who was my neurologist for over eleven years. He's an outstanding doctor and significantly advocated for me when I was applying to continue to receive the federal Disability Tax Credit. The default when applying for any kind of benefits appears to be rejection of the first application and hope that the applicant doesn't have the energy and insight to make an appeal—at least that's my somewhat snarky interpretation. I've said on numerous occasions, "Filling out disability forms is so disabling!" Having a doctor share in my frustrations and advocate for me isn't something I take for granted.

My last appointment with Dr. Marriott was in the summer of 2021, and I didn't meet my next MS doctor until October 2023. This was the longest I've gone without a neurology appointment since my diagnosis. However, Dr. Saab was worth the wait. We feel as if we hit the jackpot with him on my medical team. He's a powerful combination of knowledge, dedication, excellent bedside manner, and being down-to-earth.

Will the Third Disease-Modifying Therapy Be a Charm?
My skin suffered severely from injection site reactions, and there's permanent evidence on it of the many times I've had needles on my abdomen and legs. As a result, Dr. Marriott suggested switching to a third disease-modifying therapy, Avonex. It's injected intramuscularly once per week rather than subcutaneously three times per week, as I'd been used to with Rebif and Betaseron. The only other first-line therapy I could have tried was Copaxone, which is a synthetic drug given subcutaneously every day. Obviously, Copaxone wouldn't have been a good choice for me, since we were aiming to reduce the number of injections I was getting for the sake of my skin.

I tolerated the actual injections of Avonex well, but I experienced flu-like symptoms for twenty-four hours after each injection. This meant at least one day per week was a complete write-off for me with extreme fatigue and muscle aches.

Second-Line Therapy
Due to my intolerance of the first-line therapies, I was offered my choice of three different second-line therapies. Two of these are in pill form, and the third is an infusion given monthly. Two of the therapies wouldn't have been suitable. One

had a contraindication that came to light after a blood test, and gastrointestinal discomfort was a common side effect with the other. I wasn't keen to add to the trouble I already had with my digestive system from IBS. The winner was a medication called Gilenya, which is taken orally every day.

My last major relapse was in 2014, which also marked the last time I was given a short course of high-dose prednisone. I haven't had any notable relapses since I started treatment on Gilenya early in 2015. YAY!

I do continue to have daily symptoms, which include fatigue, spasticity and tone in my legs, ones related to elimination, and neuropathic pain. I also experience chronic symptoms like my annoying friend, Itchy Spot, on my back out of my reach, as well as foot drop in my right leg. I wear a brace called an ankle-foot orthosis (AFO) and am sometimes asked about it. It's fun for me when people inquire about the AFO because I'd rather address their curiosity than have them wonder and make assumptions. In the majority of cases, they don't expect to find out that a chronic neurological disease is behind it. When I want to be sassy, I might respond to their query with, "I've had multiple sclerosis for twenty years, and this is all I have to show for it!" I usually tell people that my foot doesn't believe in itself and then go on to show how I can lift my left toes higher than my right ones.

My favourite encounter with someone asking about my brace occurred at our nephew's wedding. I felt conspicuous, as my bold blue brace and black Nike runners with contrasting white swoop didn't exactly go with my long black dress with a delicate floral pattern. A man I'd never met asked me about my injury, trying to show solidarity because he knew how I felt, considering that he'd gone through bracing after his Achilles' tendon injury. I think I set him straight on my reason for the AFO, but it was fun to believe I could come across as someone with an athletic injury rather than someone with a chronic disease.

My Favourite Rollercoaster

After I'd had MS for a decade, we found ourselves on vacation in Florida. I was dealing with a motor relapse at the time, and walking around all the amusement parks was tiring. We found ourselves at SeaWorld, where there are a number of rollercoasters, including the thrilling *Manta*. This ride has the cars attached to a track at the top rather than on one underneath. It goes through a variety of dips, turns, and loops, all while providing an amazing view as riders get a different perspective while looking down past their feet. My family was concerned about how I would fare on such a wild ride. I have said that *Manta* was a great leveller. For the first time on that trip and since my diagnosis, I was able to forget about my abnormal neurology. There was only time for fun, as I enjoyed the same exhilarating experience as everyone else on the ride. I wasn't being robbed of anything, and I was a participant, not a bystander. Furthermore, I was having the time of my life.

Multiple sclerosis impacted me in many ways, but the depletion of my energy reserves has been the most significant of all.

Takeaways

- Go on rollercoasters.
- Where appropriate, I recommend allowing children to be involved and encouraged to ask questions when it comes to a family member's health experience.
- Make use of rewards programs offered!
- Don't blame yourself or apologize for circumstances out of your control.
- Embrace levity and laughter amidst trials and troubles.
- Swallow your pride; your life will become richer and your relationships more genuine.
- Take care of yourself in order to be better able to take care of your loved ones.
- Let go of ideals and accept that you can't control everything, like dictating when you'll get pregnant. Sometimes a different version of ideal is waiting for you.
- Be gracious when people say things that seem insensitive to you or strike a nerve. You won't regret holding back on crabby comments.
- Learn to pivot. (For fans of the sitcom *Friends*, think like Ross.) Something that works at one time may not continue to do so indefinitely. Be open to change if needed.

Five
TIRED OF BEING TIRED

In "Not My Favourite Rollercoaster," I mentioned fatigue being one of the top complaints of MS patients. People often think they can relate, because everyone knows what it's like to be tired or even to want to take a nap. MS fatigue gives me a feeling of total exhaustion. It can feel like there are sandbags across my body, pinning me down and keeping me horizontal.

Fatigue Really Gets on My Nerves

When I first understood what was happening at the nerve level, I began to understand why I felt so exhausted all the time. When demyelination occurs, the protective myelin sheath around a nerve becomes damaged or scarred. In order for the brain to send messages across one of these nerves, they have to be pushed over the scarred areas; the messages don't just cruise easily along the highways of the nervous system, the network of nerves in our bodies. More effort is required to send messages, and some messages just don't make it. Hearing how all this works—more like does *not* work—gave me insight into the fact that my brain needed to use more effort to communicate with other parts of my body. No wonder I felt like Every. Single. Thing. was such a big effort. Even my brain was working harder.

I also experience physical fatigue in the sense that my muscles themselves get tired. In these cases, it's clear that messages are being slowed down and not arriving efficiently at the target muscle. My experience with foot drop in my right leg is an example of this. This kind of physical fatigue contributes to overall feelings of exhaustion. It should be noted that the muscle fatigue I experience with MS differs from the sore muscles one might get following a workout.

Fatigue may also be the result of comorbidities, or coexisting diseases and conditions. Clinical depression and chronic migraine are two examples of ones I deal with, and they can both compound MS fatigue.

As anyone who has had an infant or puppy in the house will know, interruptions to your night can certainly make you tired the next day. One of the extra-special nuances of my MS is how often I get up at night to use the bathroom. In addition to the bladder issue I will discuss in the next chapter, I have overactive bladder. Thanks to the guidance from the MS clinic, I've become diligent about drinking six to eight glasses of water each day. There's a running tally in my head every day as I keep track of the volume of my water intake for each twenty-four-hour period.

My overactive bladder is mainly a nuisance during my nights. There have been nights when I've gotten up every hour or two to relieve myself. As you can imagine, not ever falling into a deep slumber can make a person rather tired the next day. I will sometimes sleep in like a teenager, as it can take me until mid to late morning to feel alert enough to start my day. At minimum, most nights I'm up two to three times.

Finally, medications can affect sleep. As you may gather from what I've described, I'm on a fair number of prescriptions. Believe it or not, I could be on more if I were to treat everything impacting me. Like apps, there's almost always a drug for that! I do carefully consider each prescription I take and look at the benefits versus the risks as well as the potential side effects. I've tried multiple medications that weren't worth the side effects, and I've chosen to put up with whatever the issue is instead of taking a drug that could potentially provide relief from some symptoms.

Serial Napper

After I told my class about my MS diagnosis, I freely shared the news with others, including our extended families. Up until this point, I had asked even Derksen5 to keep the MS news confidential.

Our extended families now knew about my diagnosis. At an aunt's funeral, I was sitting next to Kevin's cousin during the reception. I explained to him how MS impacted me in the area of fatigue and that it was the reason for my exit from classroom teaching. I must have sounded apologetic about my need for daily afternoon repose, because he looked at me and said, "Robyn, if I could take a nap every day, I totally would!" My first reaction was appreciation for him *normalizing* my situation and validating me in a way. I love the concept of normalizing, and I think I did feel some reassurance, knowing daytime snoozing was not a weird thing in the eyes of others. However, there was something key in what he said that rubbed me the wrong way when I pondered it further. He said, "If I *could* take a nap every day." Somehow it felt as if he were suggesting I was indulging in a luxury. My fatigue made me eligible for long-term disability benefits, and my job became getting the rest I *needed*, not just naps that would be *nice to indulge in*. I love this cousin, and I doubt he even remembers the conversation. I'm confident his intent was to be helpful, and before I unnecessarily replayed the conversation, that's exactly how I received it. It can be unproductive to overanalyze what people say. At the same time, it's good to try to anticipate how we might come across to others and avoid making comments that could minimize someone's experience.

> *It's good to try to anticipate how we might come across to others and avoid making comments that could minimize someone's experience.*

I went to great lengths to make sure I had the rest I needed. I have napped in many people's bedrooms or on their couches and became quite bold early on about asking if I could do just that. This was necessary when circumstances dictated that Claire and I wouldn't be home to activate our *Franklin* video routine. I was determined not to let my need for rest interfere with opportunities for Claire to have meaningful experiences away from home. Napping in strange places was a small price to pay to facilitate fun for my favourite little girl.

I found myself napping in many noisy scenarios. These included Claire's friend's house with four children playing in adjacent rooms, our parents' bedrooms with Christmas gatherings in full swing as cousins celebrated being together, and at the family cottage, with a revolving door of beachgoers returning for food and bathroom breaks. I wish I had learned earlier to have a more relaxed mindset, even if I wasn't able to get my ideal amount of sleep.

FOMO

I am easily susceptible to FOMO, or fear of missing out. As it turns out, when a mom naps every afternoon, memorable and laughter-filled moments may still be experienced by her family. This became especially apparent in the early MS days when Claire was a young child. I would often hear people referencing something that happened during my nap time. When I asked what they were talking about, I gained clarity: all the epic amusement at the heart of these conversations happened *while I was sleeping*, because that was when I donned my invisibility cloak and disappeared from interactions that my pre-MS self would have participated in. Missing out was something I needed to learn to accept as a consequence of self-care.

Take a Pill, Robyn

Fatigue was definitely my primary complaint in the early days, aside from the rollercoaster ride caused by all the relapses and remissions. Being exhausted was a constant, and the medical team at the MS clinic wanted to help me; their assistance came in the form of a prescription for Alertec. I was so hopeful it would make a difference, but I wasn't on it long thanks to experiencing some of the worst headaches I've ever endured. I just couldn't continue with a side effect like that. It's hard to know if there was any improvement with fatigue while I was battling how weary the headaches were making me feel.

About a decade later, I was under the care of Dr. Marriott. He felt it was worth another attempt at addressing my fatigue with medication, and this time amantadine was prescribed. I started the new drug in August 2012. Perhaps there was a placebo effect, or perhaps it really did help for a time. I remember that my low energy didn't interfere with my ability to attend a funeral out of province and the associated gatherings that took place. Another possibility is that I was running on a bit of adrenaline. Eventually, intolerable side effects became evident. My baseline blood pressure tends to be slightly lower than normal, and amantadine seemed to be exacerbating that condition. This side effect of increased hypotension and therefore decreased energy had the opposite effect of what we were hoping to achieve. Being even more tired made the decision to discontinue taking it an easy one.

Occupational Therapy

A major breakthrough came in 2014 when I first saw an occupational therapist. Kevin was along for the appointment when Dr. Marriott said there was one other thing we could try for fatigue: occupational therapy. At that point, Kevin felt great relief and perhaps a bit of exasperation. He commented, probably just for my ears to hear, "You mean there's a *non*-pharmaceutical option! Why didn't we start there?" I think I know why, and it can be summed up in two words: human nature. We naturally like the idea of a quick fix to a problem, and when medication is presented with the hope it may correct something that has been a struggle, we can easily gravitate to that perceived solution. The non-pharmacological option puts the ball in the patient's court with an expectation that the fatigued person will do the required work to make a difference. The MS clinic was likely used to this possible trend in patient preferences.

Dr. Marriott referred me to Marvelous Melissa, who works with MS clinic patients. One of her roles is to counsel her clients about strategies they can use to mitigate problems associated with fatigue. It was an effort to get to my occupational therapy appointments with her. It required a fair amount of time on the appointment day to bus to the hospital, have an hour-long session, and bus home. My times with Melissa were almost like emotional therapy; we talked through so many aspects of my life. As a result, it's possible these meetings were also psychologically taxing. I know they were valuable to me because it was taking part of my day I would normally be napping, required a lot of me emotionally, and homework on my part was expected.

An interesting activity was an assessment of all the different sensory inputs I experience and how each of them affects my energy. If I said watching TV was a relaxing activity for me, Melissa might probe to find out what kind of shows I was viewing. Were they busy, with rapidly changing lighting and fast-moving plots? Was there a large dynamic range in the audio track? She showed me how audio inputs tend to be draining on me, as well as anything challenging my photosensitivity (negative reaction to light). Intricate or fast-moving plots could also strain me cognitively. I enjoy cerebral challenges, but intense thinking is better suited to times other than ones when I'm meant to be resting and recharging. I wasn't surprised that activities requiring large amounts of visual and auditory inputs would be taxing, given the effect they have on my headaches. I also found it helpful to receive guidance on avoiding straining myself mentally at rest times.

Melissa had me look at how I structure my time as well. I planned out days and weeks down to the hour and minute to make sure I wasn't overextending myself. She also taught me to appreciate a good rest, even if it wasn't a big nap. After that, when I was feeling spent, it was almost supper time, and I was on the verge of being hangry, I'd go into my bedroom with the lights low and just lie down without worrying about how supper was being made or what was required of me. It was humbling to see Kevin and Claire pick up a lot of the slack in order to give me the rest I needed. More than once when I was making supper I ended up in tears and had trouble articulating why I was so emotional over what appeared to be an easy and straightforward task. Simply, I was overwhelmed and needed to find ways to ask for help. I felt guilty about not being able to follow through with making meals and doing other things for my small family. When I'm overwhelmed and try to do something in the kitchen, it's a complete disaster.

Kevin is so efficient in the kitchen; I have likened him to a whirlwind spinning rapidly from one task to the next. Being around that kind of energy and fast pace probably tires me out even more. Sometimes Claire also feels she needs to tap out and just let Kevin do his thing. When I feel that the skills required to be in the kitchen and prepare a meal exceed my abilities, I try to find something else productive to do that will still contribute to the family. Should I make rice for the meal? Can I find ingredients people need? I've been willing to cut vegetables, but Kevin's knife skills and the speed at which he can cut up food usually make the chopping tasks obvious ones to assign to him. Should I catch up on reconciling our credit cards and bank statements, or are there items in the accounts receivable or accounts payable departments of our family business that require attention? And when we're having people over and I'm too tired to really do anything meaningful in the kitchen, I self-assign the job of folding the napkins into party hats. I tend to be self-deprecating, making fun of my "dumb" contributions, but I keep hearing people tell me how much they appreciate the efforts I make. And I always need to stay on top of my self-talk, trying to eliminate words like *dumb* or *pathetic* to describe myself or my efforts.

A strategy I use is to focus on what I've accomplished and not on what I planned but didn't do. A debrief from the day could look something like this: "I slept in until eleven. I didn't get the shower cleaned. I got too hot making the beef, stirring it over a hot stove, and someone else had to take over. *Again!* I didn't exercise today." When I let that kind of negative talk spill out of my mouth, Claire often reminds me to focus on what I *have* done. It's striking that she had the same insight as the occupational therapist, because that's the field she's hoping to get her master's degree in. A more positive reflection on my day might sound something like: "I took care of myself and allowed myself to sleep in, remembering that the period following a migraine is often characterized by exhaustion. I prayed for people going through a hard time and took a moment to make them a personalized card. I checked in on our financial situation and made sure there was enough money in all the right accounts. I taught piano to a high school student and provided her with rare one-on-one instruction, genuinely encouraging her in her musical progress and as she navigates high school life. Oh, and I combed the pup." That's better!

Much of what Melissa taught me was about time management, sourcing out ways others could help me, and then swallowing my pride and asking for help; she also brought to my attention ways in which my attitude and outlook needed to be adjusted. It was a rich and affirming experience to meet with her every six weeks or so. It was well worth the interruption to my day and the effort to bus to the rehabilitation hospital where she worked. When I reflect on that time, it was as if she kept finding new approaches to saying, "There is *a lot* you do that's of great value to your family. Plan to manage your time and activities logically. And even if you can't lie down and sleep, make sure you find a quiet place, without stressful stimuli, to recharge. Be positive about who you are and what you contribute to your family and the people in your life."

Another way Melissa helped me was by equipping me to graciously respond, with my dignity intact, to a question I sometimes get asked. As North Americans, we don't always excel at conversation and asking the best questions. Why are we often preoccupied with finding out what someone does for a living? When that question would be asked of me, I'd often respond with, "Well, I have MS and experience a lot of fatigue, so I'm on long-term disability."

One day, a lovely woman from church wanted to get to know me more and asked me, "So, Robyn, how do you spend your time?" I gave an apologetic answer, referencing my MS fatigue because I felt I suddenly needed to account for how I spend all my hours and minutes. This woman wasn't asking for or expecting an account of my activities; she sincerely wanted to get to know me and asked an innocent question. My self-consciousness about not doing as much as what I think is normal made this conversation feel awkward—for me. When I told Melissa about this, she asked me, "Why did you tell her about MS and disability right away? Those are not things you need to share in a small-talk part of a conversation."

What followed was the completion of an exercise I never wanted to do. We took time and looked at each activity I participated in over a day and a week. I was resistant to doing this because I didn't want to give an account of how I spend my time, fearing it would seem pathetic hearing how little I could manage. However, Melissa affirmed me by summarizing all the ways she saw me contributing to my family, friends, and church. She proposed that I basically tell people, "I'm a piano teacher, and I manage and organize our household." I didn't need to apologetically mention the small student roster. I am a piano teacher, and that's a valid and wonderful thing to be. I started looking at my piano teaching differently, and I think I have developed a great piano studio; I now feel honoured to have this fabulous job and, in turn, have become more invested in the work I do. Also, Kevin really appreciates the way I keep on top of our accounts.

Glutton for Punishment

Shocking information ahead: Eight years after trying amantadine and approximately fifteen years after trialing Alertec, I considered another prescription for fatigue. In August 2020, at my annual neurology appointment, one of the options for me to consider was modafinil, for my fatigue. If there are any pharmacists reading this, you probably want to shout, "RED FLAG! Modafinil is the same drug as Alertec, and you said you had unbearable migraines when you tried Alertec." All of that is true, and I thank you for your concern. The medical team made me aware of this, but they explained that the headache side effect usually diminishes with time as the patient's body adjusts to the medication. I decided I was up for the challenge and determined to muscle through longer than my brief trial the first time.

I started on a low dose, definitely had *brain pain*, but noticed that the headaches were diminishing by the end of the first week. This pattern continued for another three weeks, as each week my dose increased until I was finally at the one proven to be most effective. The fact that I persevered is a reflection of the positive results I was getting from the drug. I keep a careful record of when I get headaches and how I treat them. The pre-modafinil headache frequency compared with my experience after being on the full dose didn't reveal any remarkable differences. I was ecstatic. I endured some rough headaches to finally have some help with my exhaustion.

Thankfully, I had seen Melissa already and made wise decisions with my extra alertness. Notice that I said "extra alertness" and not "more energy." There's a distinction. I could stay awake for more hours in a day, but I wasn't scurrying around with a sudden ability to move faster, get to more places, and enjoy stronger muscles.

It became possible for me to have a busy day and not stop for a nap. That was an incredible feeling! However, I was wise in realizing I still needed restful downtime. If I pushed myself too hard, I would crash. There have been some no-nap days when I tried to be a superhero, and Kevin has come home to find me in bed at supper time, trying to get the rest I should have stopped to take earlier in the day. My fatigue isn't cured with this, but how sharp I feel most days has definitely increased. I'm usually in bed for ten to twelve hours each night—minus the bathroom interruptions. And it's only on days after a good night of sleep that I can push myself and manage without a nap. Could I return to full-time classroom teaching? Not a chance. This is a case of *better than*, not *all better*. My alertness is better than it used to be but certainly not all better, and my physical energy is still low.

Take This Lesson to the Bank

When I was a teenager, I was given an assignment in biology class to research and give an oral presentation on a disease of my choosing. The disease I opted for was myalgic encephalomyelitis, or ME. My aunt had already been living with ME for a number of years, and she welcomed a visit from me to talk about the illness. The most common symptom ME patients face is incapacitating fatigue. Everyone in the extended family knew Auntie Maryrose got really tired. I remember her disappearing to a bedroom upstairs to rest during a family gathering. No one in the family could comprehend the impact it had on her, aside from my wonderful and caring Uncle Bill.

Over thirty years ago, she explained something to me about living with chronic fatigue that I remember to this day; it has been helpful for me as I contend with my own fatigue. She described how she managed her energy. There might be a day when she felt better than usual and had more energy than she was used to. The temptation would be to use all that energy to make up for lost time and tackle as many tasks as possible. However, if that approach were taken, she'd likely crash during the following day, days, or weeks. Therefore, it is best not to use up all of the perceived extra energy. This approach is a strategy to prevent low times.

If she had a big event coming up, Auntie Maryrose would bank her energy. She would proactively spend many days lying low to conserve energy; then on event day, she'd be able to pull from those reserves. And the days following the big event would require extra rest.

Apparently, I'm not an excellent student and haven't always applied the lessons she shared with me. One day in the fall of 2022, I felt much better than usual. It was exactly three weeks after I'd tested positive for COVID-19. I don't know what I was thinking when I decided it would be a great occasion to *do all the things*.

I woke up earlier than usual and couldn't fall back to sleep. Happily, Claire was up for the day and getting ready to go to university. I had breakfast with her and then walked with her to her bus stop. When I left the bus stop, I chose to complete the walk around the block instead of taking a more direct route home. It was a long walk for me, but it felt terrific to be able to do it. Next, I headed to one of the labs in the city to have my quarterly blood work done. After that, I went to a little shop to buy gluten-free pizza crusts to allow me to participate in the pizza night being planned at our house a couple of days later. I had a frustrating time trying to find street parking, which is a scenario that is sure to wear on me. But I was able to complete the task and even had the opportunity to pick up some of Big Sister's favourite muffins.

My next errand took me to the grocery store. Kevin does most of the grocery shopping for our family these days, and I really wanted to give him a break. As it happened, it was a bigger shopping trip than just a replenishment of our milk, egg, and bread caches. Some of the items were heavy, which made pushing the cart a big effort. This particular store doesn't bag purchases for customers, so I proceeded to do that once everything had been scanned and paid for.

I was ready to go when I realized that my jacket had been covering up some produce. In my wisdom to remove my jacket to avoid overheating, I had accidentally hidden the sweet potatoes under it. I'm glad I noticed before I left the store because my conscience would never allow me to be a yam-stealer—particularly not on the day I had already accidentally driven in the bus-only rapid transit lanes before my first errand.

When I got home, Kevin got all the groceries from the trunk and put them away. Thank you, Husband. Then I decided to make homemade bread. A couple in our care group[1] had recently moved, and I earnestly wanted to make a meal for them but didn't have the energy to do so. However, making bread doesn't require me to stand by a hot stove or follow an unfamiliar recipe. As I was making the bread, Big Sister showed up to pick up her muffins. We had a great visit, but it did cut into the nap I was planning to have while the dough was rising. After she left, I headed to bed and explained to Kevin what needed to happen to finish preparing the bread. He kindly formed the dough into loaves after the first rise was complete and put them in the oven after the second rise. In the end, I was able to give a loaf of homemade bread to our care group friends. It felt good to be able to do something to encourage them during their move, even if it wasn't a full meal or physical help with moving their belongings.

This was not a regular day for me; I pushed myself beyond the limits of my energy. I think feeling *better than* I had when I had COVID-19 had tricked me into thinking that I was *all better*. No, Robyn. You still have MS. Silly girl.

Fatigue has impacted me in significant ways, and I haven't always been fabulous at learning from the past. Managing fatigue is itself tiring and requires regular positive mental shifts to cope with well. Those positive shifts are another aspect in which I have proven to be a slow learner.

As difficult as this symptom has been, there have been a couple of "benefits"—literally. I qualified for various disability benefits as a direct result of the disabling effect of fatigue.

---

[1] Our church has a number of care groups. These are small groups of congregants who meet together regularly to study the Bible, pray together, and encourage each other.

Takeaways

- Be bold, especially if it benefits your child, with some self-care thrown in.
- Be willing to put in some work and not rely on quick fixes. Ironically, the work I needed to do to understand my fatigue resulted in more rest for me in the long run.
- Don't be apologetic about your circumstances, limits, abilities, or capacity.
- Be willing to revisit solutions—the second or third time might be charming.
- Learn from the past.

Six
A TALE OF THREE BENEFITS

What follows is a discussion of financial matters and calculations. These are the kinds of things my brother-in-law, Julio, enjoys. I'm including this detailed portrait of my benefits to give you an idea of how tiresome it can be to manage and understand these matters and their implications. At times, I've explained this to interested people like Julio, and they seem to find it fascinating. These are special people.

Long-Term Disability

Little did I know what a steep learning curve I'd be on as I navigated the world of insurance for people with disabilities. I've made reference to the long-term disability (LTD) benefits I receive. Those were the first benefits I applied for. What I didn't realize when I applied for these is that the people handling my file would operate with predetermined responses and wouldn't be replying to my request on a personal, human level. I've heard it explained that the first response from an insurance company is often to decline the application.

I mentioned in "Not My Favourite Rollercoaster" how filling out forms for disability benefits felt disabling. Insurance companies ask you a plethora of questions and also ask for medical evidence. Usually getting this medical evidence is not only time-consuming and tedious but also expensive. I was eventually approved for LTD benefits, but the insurance company wasn't prepared to allow me to be on full-time long-term disability; they needed to see me make an attempt to go back to work.

Often when people are put on short- or long-term disability, the insurance company gets involved in trying to help them rejoin the workforce. I felt frustrated as I learned that I'd have to fill out a "progress report" biannually, again with medical evidence, to determine whether I was still eligible to receive benefits. This report is not nearly as involved as the initial application for long-term disability benefits, but it still feels like an inconvenient and tedious nuisance. I couldn't understand why they were putting me through this process; certainly people in the life and disability insurance industry would know MS is not a disease that improves in time! Were they expecting a complete turnaround and that I would magically be full of vim and vigour and ready to face the heavy demands of middle years teaching again?

I remember filling out the forms and adding a letter with some snarky remarks about how I was sure they must understand that MS is a progressive disease and that I shouldn't be expected to be making great strides in recovery. Little did I know how much of a formality these biannual reassessments actually are.

Over time, I learned to tell myself to react logically and not emotionally. Now when I face those forms, I just answer the questions, giving them no more and no less information than they ask for. When I was first approved for long-term disability benefits, my doctor and I painted a picture of how my increased fatigue made returning to full-time teaching impossible for me.

How was my LTD benefit calculated? The simple answer is that they looked at my gross income from my teaching position before going on medical leave and multiplied it by two-thirds to arrive at a number that would later be referred to as the *sum of all sources* (SOAS). This roughly translated to what my net income would have been pre-disability. This became my baseline number for the benefit I continue to receive monthly from long-term disability insurance. This is a non-taxable amount, so it continues to represent my net income from 2002.

To illustrate how this actually plays out, I'll use the amount of $1,000 to represent my gross monthly income before my disability claim. If that were the case, the SOAS would be $667.67. All calculations and amounts in this chapter are proportionate to the benefits I actually receive, but the starting point of $1,000 is hypothetical. For all calculations and possible scenarios, the sum of all sources is always the starting point. This number never changes—it's always referencing back to 67 per cent of my salary before becoming disabled.

There are three possible scenarios when considering only my long-term disability benefit:

1. I am not working. This was the case when I first qualified for LTD while on maternity leave.
2. I am working and earning in excess of the "additional allowable earnings" amount the insurance company calculates, which increases annually. This occurred after my maternity leave when I went back to teaching part-time. For this situation, we became familiar with another term—all source max (ASM). The ASM is the most I'm allowed to earn from LTD and any additional income I earn from employment. If the sum of all sources

plus my employment earnings exceeds the ASM, my LTD benefit will be reduced by the amount of the excess. If I earn $500 from employment, and the additional allowable earnings amount is $100, the excess deducted would be $400. The $500 I earned is $400 more than the $100 of additional allowable earnings.
3. The final situation involves receiving the long-term disability benefit and earning income that doesn't surpass the allowable earnings calculated for me. This is what happens now with my work as a piano teacher because I don't earn enough to exceed the allowable earnings amount. When my benefit and earnings don't exceed the all source max, I receive the sum of all sources.

Applying for LTD is a tedious and sometimes emotional process. Aside from leaving the house to attend the necessary medical appointments, my efforts were unseen outside of our home. Navigating this new world of disability insurance benefits was often a lonely, exhausting, and frustrating experience.

Canada Pension Plan

When I was approved for long-term disability benefits, I was told that I could be asked to apply for Canada Pension Plan (CPP) disability benefits anytime. After four months back at work in a part-time capacity following my maternity leave, it was decided I had given it the "old college try," and I would be going on medical leave. It was then that the LTD insurance company asked me to apply for CPP disability benefits. Only people who have contributed to the Canada Pension Plan are eligible for pension and disability benefits through this plan. Most working Canadians contribute to CPP. I will receive this benefit until I'm sixty-five, at which time I'll continue to receive CPP, but as a retirement benefit.

I appreciated my application being approved without needing to appeal, and I continue to enjoy the benefit of not needing to reapply or prove with medical evidence that I'm still disabled enough to receive it. With both the CPP and LTD benefit, I'm required to report if my condition changes substantially such that I would be able to return to working in a greater capacity. Given the prolonged and progressive nature of MS, this has not happened and will not happen, apart from a miraculous intervention.

It was a welcome surprise to learn that Claire would also receive a benefit from CPP. Claire, as my dependent child, was entitled to an amount of about one-third of what I received through CPP. The excitement over this revelation didn't last long. I learned quickly that my LTD insurance company would be deducting both my benefit as well as Claire's from what they paid out to me. However, adding the CPP disability benefit into the mix came with an advantage over receiving compensation solely through the long-term disability benefit: unlike my LTD benefit, the CPP benefit is indexed for inflation.

Now that I was receiving a benefit from another source, the CPP benefit was subtracted from the *sum of all sources* to determine how much less LTD benefit would be paid out. The amount of the CPP benefit deducted from the *sum of all sources* is the CPP benefit originally assigned to me when I was approved for it in 2004. Unlike my LTD benefit, the proceeds from CPP are taxable and indexed for inflation. Thankfully, my LTD benefit is not further reduced by the cost-of-living increase component of my CPP benefit.

The fact that my LTD benefit wouldn't grow with inflation was written into the policy book I received when I first contributed to the group insurance plan with my work. It wasn't something we had considered looking into when we were first given literature about the group insurance plan, which eventually granted me LTD benefits, because such implications weren't high on our minds. To have a policy indexed for inflation is considerably more expensive than one that is not, and when someone is contributing to a group plan, there isn't room to tweak the plan in the way an individual plan might be customized. Plans outside of a group policy are more expensive and will probably come with a requirement for full disclosure of any pre-existing medical conditions, along with medical evidence of good health.

When Claire turned eighteen, she was in for a treat. As of the month of her eighteenth birthday, the child's portion of the CPP disability benefit was paid directly to her. She's eligible to receive this benefit until she's twenty-five, as long as she's enrolled in post-secondary education on a full-time basis. I guess she's finally being compensated for all those times she had to suffer through watching *Franklin* videos while I slept. Claire *should* be rewarded for her wonderful attitude toward her disabled mother and all the ways she has helped me practically and emotionally.

> Claire should be rewarded for her wonderful attitude toward her disabled mother and all the ways she has helped me practically and emotionally.

Speaking of her wonderful attitude, when I told her she'd be receiving the child's portion, she immediately said, "Well, I'll just pay that amount back to you every month." Kevin and I were happy for her to receive the benefit, and she accepted her good fortune.

My current reality consists of the sum of all sources from my long-term disability benefit (minus the 2004 CPP benefit amount), CPP disability benefits, and additional earnings I receive through teaching piano. The all source max has essentially become irrelevant, as my remunerations from teaching piano aren't enough to cause me to exceed the ASM. The additional allowable earnings amount increases each year, but my energy for teaching piano has decreased. I have fewer students than I used to, and I haven't been close to reaching the ASM for a number of years.

Disability Tax Credit

The third benefit I receive works differently. With LTD and CPP disability, my fatigue was the major complaint I presented with. However, fatigue is not how a person qualifies for the Canadian federal Disability Tax Credit, or DTC. We became aware of the DTC when we switched our modest investment portfolio over to financial planner Todd Reimer. At our first meeting, he asked us if I'd ever applied for the DTC. When he described it, I didn't think I would be a candidate. There are specific criteria for eligibility. The Government of Canada explains on their website:

> *You may be eligible for the DTC if a medical practitioner certifies that you have a severe and prolonged impairment in 1 of the categories, significant limitations in 2 or more categories, or receive therapy to support a vital function.*[2]

These categories are as follows:
- Walking
- Mental functions
- Dressing
- Feeding
- Eliminating (bowel or bladder functions)
- Hearing
- Speaking
- Vision
- Life-sustaining therapy

Of course, the first thing I did was scan the list for anything to do with fatigue, because that was how I was used to qualifying for benefits. Ironically, I was disappointed to not be disabled enough, or at least not the right kind

---

[2] "Disability tax credit (DTC)," Government of Canada, accessed September 17, 2024, https://www.canada.ca/en/revenue-agency/services/tax/individuals/segments/tax-credits-deductions-persons-disabilities/disability-tax-credit/eligible-dtc.html.

of disabled. However, upon further reflection, one category caught my eye: eliminating.

I've had both bladder and bowel challenges since early in the course of my disease. As is typical with pregnancy, I experienced constipation, which continued after the MS diagnosis. Given that the first signs of MS coincided with the first signs of pregnancy, the constipation could believably have been caused by either "condition," or perhaps both.

I didn't realize that I could have the types of bladder issues I had until I experienced them. I'm constantly learning new and strange facts about how our bodies work, or don't work. The bladder is far more complex than I ever imagined. I thought the only bladder problem would be incontinence, or *going when you don't want to go*. I was mistaken. Our bladders have muscles that help us *not go when we don't want to go* and other muscles that help us *go when we want to go*. I've had substantial trouble with the latter group of muscles. I have what's called *bladder hesitancy*. To make a long story short, it takes me an "inordinate amount of time with the processes of elimination." Bingo. That's how I qualified for the DTC.

When you apply for the DTC, they don't just take your word for it. You need medical evidence. Since the MS clinic was aware of the bladder hesitancy, they referred me to a urologist, Dr. Dave Maharaj. He had me undergo a flow test in which I voided into a device that measured the speed of urine output over time. When I had completed the test, I went back into Dr. Maharaj's office, where he showed me the results. It was evident from the test that urine hesitancy was indeed a substantial issue—there was a lot of starting and stopping.

He also sent me for an ultrasound of my bladder and kidneys. We discussed the results, and he didn't find anything remarkable about my bladder but casually mentioned that I have a kidney stone in my right kidney. *Wait, what?* Would I not be writhing in pain if I had a kidney stone? Apparently not always. Many people have kidney stones and are completely oblivious to their existence. It's only when the stones move, especially into a ureter, that the pain associated with kidney stones occurs. Still, it did feel troubling to know I had a kidney stone.

All the appointments mentioned above occurred in 2010. We didn't hear about the DTC from Mr. Reimer until 2011 or later. When we began to pursue applying for it, I visited Dr. Maharaj again. He kindly filled out the medical evidence section of the application.

But my application was not approved.

I find the drama of being rejected and then needing to appeal exhausting. I imagine many people give up out of DFF (Disability Form Fatigue). It's not just the time it takes to fill out the forms but also the time and precious energy it takes to go to the required medical appointments. After I finished pouting about it, I got to work on the appeal. I proactively did something exhilarating, which I would highly recommend everyone do at least once in their lives. I set a stopwatch every single time I voided over a period of three days. I brought my voiding journal to my appointment with Dr. Maharaj to discuss the appeal to the DTC decision. I explained to him that it appeared the reason I was denied was because he checked the box that said I took a "significant amount of time" rather than an "inordinate amount of time" in the processes of elimination. My voiding journal revealed to him that my first and last voids of the day can easily take at least twenty minutes. The voids in between generally took a long time, just not quite twenty minutes. Dr. Maharaj was happy to check the "inordinate" box, and now "inordinate" has become a favourite word in our house. We are grateful for this doctor's help, because after the appeal, my application was approved!

Frustratingly, the DTC needs to be re-applied for every number of years. To date, I have applied three times and had to appeal the first two times. I was shocked and relieved (pardon the pun) to have had my application accepted without needing to appeal the last time I applied. Perhaps the Canada Revenue Agency (CRA) caught on that my doctors meant it when they said my condition is prolonged (i.e., chronic and not expected to improve).

So what does the DTC give me? The answer to this question is twofold.

1. The DTC is a non-refundable tax credit, which can reduce the amount of income tax we pay. When we file our income tax, I have to indicate that I'm disabled and that I have a current Disability Tax Credit Certificate registered with the Canada Revenue Agency (CRA). The credit can be claimed on mine or Kevin's tax return.
2. I was given the opportunity to contribute to a Registered Disability Savings Plan (RDSP), and the government added to my contribution in two ways—through the Canada Disability Savings Grant and through the Canada Disability Savings Bond. I could contribute as much as I wanted and could make contributions until the year I turned forty-nine. If I added $1,500 to my RDSP annually, I would have attracted $3,500 in contributions from the federal government. If the sum was greater than $1,500 per year, the government contribution wouldn't have increased beyond $3,500. If I allotted less than $1,500 to my RDSP each year, the government portion would have been less than $3,500. Consequently, I always contributed exactly $1,500 each year until the year I turned forty-nine.

The non-refundable tax credit is welcome and certainly saves us to a small degree on our tax return, but the grant and bond contributions from the Canadian government will prove to be even more valuable long-term.

I was initially sad about my LTD benefit not being indexed for inflation, but the CPP disability benefit (which does increase with the cost of living), the CPP disability children's benefit, and the DTC perks were all welcome consolations. They certainly don't make up for the loss in wages if I consider what I would have earned had I been able to continue teaching, but I'm not complaining. I don't worry about this pay cut, and I'm proud of myself for fighting hard for the benefits I do receive.

The effort and back-and-forth involved in these benefits is taxing. It takes its toll physically because it's time-consuming and requires alert energy from me. It can also be draining mentally and emotionally, and my mental health has been fragile, especially since my MS diagnosis.

SIX: A TALE OF THREE BENEFITS

Takeaways

1. If facing daunting insurance forms, allow logic to prevail and do your best to detach yourself emotionally. Take a deep breath and approach the task on a day when you have enough physical, cognitive, and emotional energy.
2. Talk to people who have been where you are and find out what benefits are likely available to you. Keep in mind that some benefits may be an actual monetary benefit passed on to you monthly, and some may be in the form of tax relief or savings opportunities.
3. Read about possible benefits thoroughly. Avoid making assumptions about how you might qualify for compensation, because you may qualify in a way you hadn't considered at first.

Seven
IT'S ALL RIGHT TO CRY

What follows is a rough transcript of the first conversation I had with our neighbour's girlfriend.

Penny: It's great to finally meet you. Welcome to the neighbourhood!

Me: I'm so glad to meet you too. I hear Kevin has been talking to all the neighbours when he's been working here. Has Kevin been too much?

Penny: Yeah, no, of course not! He's been great. I think my boyfriend has appreciated the way he's handled the building process.

Me: Building a house has been intense. It probably doesn't help that I went off my antidepressant this year.

Penny: Ooohh, that sounds rough.

Me: Yeah, I'd been on antidepressants for about a decade and was curious to see if I could be normal without them. Lol.

Penny: I have a family member with a mental illness. Balancing the medications on top of the actual illness is super tough.

Me: I'm beginning to appreciate how much the meds really balanced the chemicals in my brain. I'm not avoiding the subject of depression, but I just noticed some cool ink on your arm. Are you working on a sleeve?

Penny: Yeah. It's going to be a family tree. The tree on my shoulder and down part of my arm is for my dad, as well as this classic car. I have plans for more, to add stuff for my mom and brother too.

Me: That's so cool. Have you seen the house yet? I can give you a tour, but I should warn you that beds are not made.

Penny: Oh, don't ever worry about that with me. Actually, I've heard that it's healthier anyway because the sun's rays kill the dust mites.

Me:	Haha. That would be helpful, perhaps, if we ever opened our curtains. I hide in dark rooms because of chronic migraine.
Penny:	I get migraines too.
Me:	I think we'll get along great. Follow me back to our place if you want the two-cent tour of the house in its messy, moving-in condition.
Penny:	I'd love to see it. We've been curious while we watched it being built.

I told Kevin about our conversation and how I had toured her through our house, including all the closets. He expressed his amazement at how much ground we covered in such a short time—small talk to mental illness to tattoos to a house tour. Kevin talks to his friends about construction and shows people the crawl space under our basement. I tend to do this—not the *talking about construction and showing people our crawl space* part, rather the *covering a lot of ground quickly* part. "Hi. My name is Robyn. I'm on citalopram. Which antidepressant are you on?" Maybe it's not quite that direct, but I'm not shy about sharing that I'm clinically depressed and happily (most of the time) medicated.

Prednisone

Whereas my physical illnesses had obvious, attention-getting symptoms, my mental illness rather sneaked up on me. In fact, at first it seemed related to MS. As mentioned in the "Rollercoaster" chapter, I've taken prednisone to shorten motor relapses multiple times. Early in my disease course, the frequency with which prednisone became a treatment was definitely higher than it was in later years for a few reasons. 1) Claire was more dependent on and demanding of me, as babies and toddlers naturally are in those early child-parent relationships. The relapses triggering a steroid prescription were more disabling and more affected my ability to care for Claire. 2) MS attacks occurred less frequently as time went on. Those first few years felt especially intense. 3) I grew to dread taking prednisone. The more often I was on it, the more determined I became to *not* resort to steroids again. I didn't control or predict with this resolve my relapses, but I did learn to just live with certain symptoms.

In the first two and a half years following my MS diagnosis, I was on prednisone at least four times. With each occurrence, it became harder to go through the steroids fiasco again. It was dramatic experiencing all the physical impacts of the treatment, but the mental and emotional components were no less significant. The few days that I took the extremely high dose weren't down days emotionally. Having energy, alertness, and a clearer cognitive presence was exhilarating at times. However, the lows during the tapering off and after the treatment course was complete got lower each time. I remember telling Kevin, "If I ever need to go on prednisone again, I want to start on antidepressants. This is just getting too hard."

Medicated

In July 2005, when I knew I'd be taking prednisone, I called Dr. Bev and asked her if I could start on an antidepressant after the steroid treatment was complete. She thought that was a reasonable course of action and wrote the appropriate prescription. It took me about two weeks to adjust to this medication and get past the extra layer of fatigue it caused. After that time, I was back to my new normal of the now-familiar MS fatigue.

Interestingly and surprisingly to me, my depression symptoms weren't overwhelming sadness or bouts of crying. My most pronounced symptom was irritability, and I'm sure that was frustrating for the two people I live with. My irritation extended beyond our family of three, and after being treated pharmaceutically for a time, I began to realize that people I had found exasperating were, in fact, lovely individuals. I would be scared to know how I must have come across in those days.

Circumstantial and clinical depression are both realities I have dealt with. I had a lot of stressors in my life preceding starting on an antidepressant, and the weight of the situations I was dealing with definitely intensified the mood disorder.

The birth of our child and start of parenthood were wonderful, but unsurprisingly, involved increases in both stress and joy. I've often said to new parents, "You will never cry, and you will never laugh so much in your life!" The moments of joy Claire has brought into our lives have astronomically outweighed any stress that parenting her has involved.

A second stressor was learning that I had a chronic health condition and subsequently discovering what it meant to live with it. This new reality was accompanied by many decisions about medications we had never faced before, as well as learning about and filing for long-term disability benefits. Honestly, the first time I was offered steroids for a motor relapse I was convinced I was experiencing the worst possible MS attack. I wasn't anticipating diplopia or other motor relapses with more debilitating symptoms. I was eager to put the attack behind me and delighted there was a proposed solution. I was also counting on my disease-modifying therapy to reduce the frequency and severity of the MS attacks. I didn't imagine being faced with so many relapses leading to prednisone treatment in a relatively short time. Everything seemed to come to a head when I faced steroids in 2005 and subsequently asked for an antidepressant. I could sum up how I was feeling in one word: overwhelmed.

Important PSA
I'm not apologizing for treating my depression pharmaceutically. Robyn-from-the-present would like to affirm Robyn-from-the-past in her decision to start medication for depression. Mood disorders should never be brushed off and should always be taken seriously. The most significant reminder I have of this is the memory of two young men who were dear to me and who took their own lives as a direct result of mental illness.

No Feelings
Aside from the initial fatigue, the biggest side effect of the antidepressant I noticed was the sense that I had no feelings anymore. I no longer felt negative or misplaced emotions and reactions such as anger and irritability, but I also found I no longer cried when crying would be an appropriate response. I went to the funeral of someone who passed away in her forties from cancer, and I didn't shed a tear. I absolutely cared, was moved, and was touched hearing about her life, but my usual crying response was missing.

Irrational Much?
In 2005, when I started on citalopram, Kevin and I didn't have cell phones. We certainly didn't have iPhones with the ability to iStalk each other. My dear spouse went out one day to do some errands and got carried away. I became worried when he wasn't home for supper. Kevin always makes sure to get three meals each day plus healthy, protein-rich snacks in between. It was out of character for him to be missing at meal time. I did what any rational wife would do—I called the police. I refrained from calling 911 but rather found the non-emergency number in an ancient document called a phone book. This is roughly how the conversation with law enforcement went:

Me: Hello. My husband is missing. It hasn't been twenty-four hours yet, and I know you only consider someone missing if it's been at least that long, but I'm really worried because he hasn't come home for supper, and he always comes home to eat.

SEVEN: IT'S ALL RIGHT TO CRY

The Law: Ma'am, that's just on TV or in the movies. Someone doesn't have to be missing for twenty-four hours or more to be considered a missing person. Have you called the hospitals?
Me: No.
The Law: I can tell you there haven't been any major traffic incidents.

Those were the highlights. I can't remember any more details from that anxious conversation I had twenty years ago. I didn't file a missing person's report; I think I felt reassured to know there hadn't been any major accidents, because that was the only possible scenario I could imagine being responsible for Kevin's absence.

Kevin arrived home feeling happy and excited to tell me about his errands. Of course, now neither of us have any recollection of what he was doing that day. All I know is he had an annoyingly reasonable account of his time away, with receipts to show for it. Unfortunately for Kevin, he couldn't announce his happiness about what he'd done for quite a while, because when he walked in the door, I blurted out, "Well, I found out I can still cry on antidepressants. Also, you should know the entertainment industry has misled us about how the police handle missing persons' reports."

Robyn, is this chapter called "It's All Right to Cry" because you cried that one time your husband was fake-missing, causing you to jump to conclusions and overreact? Thanks for the question; the crying is still coming. Now you have something to look forward to.

I was generally "happily medicated" for clinical depression, and life kept moving along. I've heard stories or seen depictions on TV of patients with mental illness feeling so good on their medication that they stop taking it, hoping they're "better" now. I'm not sure I felt that confident, but I was curious about how I would do without my antidepressant. I wanted to be "Robyn" not "Robyn-plus." After about ten years on citalopram, I tapered off the medication.

There's a great joke Little Sister tells well. I'm not sure I can do it justice in print, but I will attempt.

What's the difference between a good joke and a bad jo—Timing!

Husband Builds Me a House

My timing in taking a medication holiday was perhaps not exactly what one might consider logical. I tapered off the antidepressant around the time we started building a house. This was the second house we built, and I could have anticipated the construction process would involve extra stress in our lives.

Kevin is amazing when it comes to anything to do with houses. He and his parents have been involved in renovating or building many houses over the years. He has knowledge of every trade and each aspect of the process. We hired a general contractor for our first house-building project and were both involved in making myriad decisions. When we built the second one, Kevin acted as the general contractor and was personally involved in every decision, and he designed a house with many visible and invisible accessibility features. I completely trusted him to build our house. I literally told him, "Husband, build me a house." And he did.

I joined him and gave input in aspects such as the kitchen, appliances, and flooring. He also consulted me on paint colour and would sometimes play fun games late at night with me by asking on which wall I'd like the light switch in our bedroom closet. I confessed to him later that although I really did try to imagine walking into the closet and flicking on the light, my answer may not have been exhaustively thought out, unless it counts that I was exhausted when trying to think about how to answer. I also admitted that my instincts since moving have been to feel for the switch on the wall it isn't on. As it turns out, the decision we made late that night was essentially moot. Due to something structural, the wall I chose happens to be the only wall that really would have worked.

Clearly Kevin took care of the house-build and me at the same time, with all the special considerations he factored into our home. So why would it be a stressful time for me if he handled everything? Because we're married, and it was stressful for him to be away at "the new house" as much as he needed to be. His responsibilities abounded, and there was little I could do to help him. At the end of each day, it was hard to properly debrief, as we both felt exhausted for different reasons. At night, his mind was perpetually dreaming about the new house and making plans accordingly. I have only comprehended in part how big the weight on his shoulders was, and I appreciate his thoughtfulness and skill immensely.

OT Observations

As mentioned in the "Tired of Being Tired" chapter, I had the privilege of seeing Melissa for occupational therapy. She interacted with me over a number of sessions and made some observations that she felt were beyond her scope to address. At one of my last meetings with Melissa, she suggested I see Kamara, the social worker for the MS clinic. I turned to her and said, "Do you think I'm a little messed up?" She never used the words "a little messed up," but in her beautiful and kind way, she let me know that she thought perhaps I needed help beyond what our conversations involved.

Therapy

Soon after we moved into our new house, I had my first appointment with Kamara. It didn't take long for it to become clear that I was officially in therapy. The tears came early in the first appointment when she asked about my parents and sisters; while I shared the beautiful ways they have cared for me, it was impossible not to become emotional. I was apologetic and embarrassed by my crying, and that became a topic we discussed often.

Since I had started my drug holiday, tears were bountiful and frequent. They also started to feel inappropriate. There seemed to be no limit to my teary triggers. It was somewhat like crying at long-distance commercials; it felt worse, though. I could accept shedding tears for what I deemed logical reasons: a sad movie, hurt feelings, and hard circumstances of someone I loved. I could somewhat understand getting weepy when Claire was a goalie on her water polo team. I've heard other parents comment on how difficult it is to watch their child playing that position. When the other team fired balls at her, I was emotional, but when she made one brilliant save after another with other parents from our team bragging about our great goalie, that put me over the edge. The problem was I didn't just get teary: I cried. The most ill-suited time I ended up in tears was at one of Claire's basketball games. I literally cried just because she got possession of the ball. It felt incredibly awkward, as this was happening in a public place. I didn't inspect every parent's cheeks in the school gym, but I'm confident mine were the only wet ones.

In therapy, I brought up my concern about the inappropriate and seemingly spontaneous crying. Kamara asked me if it felt as if the incongruous crying was on par with laughing at a funeral. Yes! It felt that misplaced. I told Kamara that I was seriously considering going back on antidepressants. I was also really struggling with irritability again. She encouraged me to work through these concerns and even tried CBT (Cognitive Behavioural Therapy) to help me cope with loud chewing noises, which were getting on my nerves and making some mealtimes hard to deal with.

Kamara and I also discussed my negative self-talk. You've probably caught on that I have a tendency to feel guilty about not being able to do everything I'd like to do domestically. It's been hard for me to become less able to cook and clean to the extent I used to, which wasn't to a superior standard anyway. She

> *I'm doing the best I can with the resources I have.*

helped me look at what was in my control and what was not. We came up with a mantra together, which I still find myself reciting: I'm doing the best I can with the resources I have.

I was excited to share this with Kevin and Claire, not because it helped me defend myself to them but because it was useful for me to put matters in perspective for myself. Kevin and Claire have reasonable expectations of me and always have.

It was helpful talking through and discovering the resources available to me. It felt constructive to make plans for how I could take care of our household *with the resources I had*. I've shared my little mantra freely with many others. I'm happy to share it with the world, so feel free to adopt it for yourself. It seems to resonate with people falling anywhere on the ability to disability spectrum. Eventually, I graduated from therapy and bought myself a hot chocolate at a coffee shop on the way out to celebrate.

I wasn't "cured," but I was equipped with some tools to enable me to cope with many of the mental challenges I faced.

Dark Days

At some point after "graduating," my mood took a dark turn. I continued to be bothered by the random acts of crying and felt bitter that I couldn't enjoy Claire's baptism in a more stable mental state. Part of me blamed Kamara for not encouraging me to end my drug holiday when I brought up the subject. I mentioned that when I was first medicated for depression, I felt everything with less intensity. The upside to this was being able to speak publicly about subjects that were spiritual or personal. I would have loved to have spoken up at Claire's baptism in affirmation of the choices she's made, but I knew with my fragile emotional state, it wasn't an option.

Even though I was equipped with a great mantra to combat my negative self-talk, at some point my feelings of inadequacy built up to a point where I considered harming myself. At that point I was convinced it was time to have a frank conversation with my doctor.

My family doctor, the terrific Dr. Tadrous, is a great listener and full of compassion and professionalism. She was thorough in the questions she asked and agreed that going back on an antidepressant was appropriate. There was only one hiccup. Since I'd last been "happily medicated," I had started on the disease-modifying therapy Gilenya. There are a number of medications that interact with Gilenya, and the antidepressant I'd previously taken is one of them. Were

I to continue taking it while on Gilenya, I'd be at risk of serious complications. This meant starting a new-to-me medication.

At our house, we've often referred to my antidepressant as my happy pill. One morning at breakfast immediately after swallowing my new happy pill, I gave Kevin and Claire a huge smile and said, "It's working!" Claire was impressed at the rapid efficacy of this new treatment. Antidepressants don't work that quickly, and we all had a good laugh when I explained this to Claire. Thankfully, duloxetine did prove to be "working" in time and has been a good fit for me. I am convinced that my clinical depression is undeniable, and I won't be going on any prescription holidays anytime soon. I've been able to cry at expected times and rarely cry at illogical ones. It feels good to feel and to also have a higher sense of mental stability.

When off antidepressants, I remember putting massive effort into acting "normal" and responding to situations in a "normal" way. I was perpetually analyzing every encounter and *trying so hard* all the time. It was exhausting to have the sense that I couldn't trust myself and to be constantly policing my words and responses. I have a sarcastic sense of humour, but the sarcasm my brain defaulted to while unmedicated was not light-hearted. It was cruel and would have caused relationship damage. This time off the medication was often a lonely one with much introspection, self-doubt, confusion, and mental effort. I'm relieved I brought my mental illness into the light as I once again approached a doctor for help. I was amazed at the difference and relief I felt once being treated pharmaceutically again, and I was more convinced than ever of the chemical imbalance that often occurs in people who experience depression and other mental illnesses.

On both medications, I've still been susceptible to discouragement. I went through a time while on the first drug when Kevin noticed that I was frequently melancholy at home, brooding as I went about my day. He noticed a contrast between my interactions within our family compared to the manner in which I related to others. I imagine this was likely due to the fact that I was actively trying to be normal to fit with social expectations, and also because I let my guard down and relaxed when at home with my people. My patient husband carefully mentioned this to me, and I made an effort to be more positive at home.

However, the issue was beyond simply needing constant effort from me. Kevin recognized this and put on his Christmas list a book to help him pray strategically for his wife. My parents were quick to purchase this for him. I knew about his request for the book and was at our gathering when he received it. Even so, I didn't wonder if Kevin had been reading it. Months later, I seemed to come out of the funk I was in. It was then that Kevin told me he had been faithfully praying for me since he'd received the gift from my parents. He was indeed praying for me before reading the book, but the book gave him guidance and helped him make the decision to be regular in his prayers for me. The book was a tool, but the power was the prayer.

Are You Sure You Aren't Just Sad?

I saw a counsellor in 2023 who made me think carefully about the difference between sadness and depression. Depression is often marked by one or all of three symptoms. Often there's a change in eating habits and appetite—either eating little, with hardly any appetite, or eating more than usual without feeling satisfied. I've experienced a decrease in appetite, and for more than one reason. Change in sleep behaviour can be another sign. Someone with depression may either be sleeping a lot more or might be having trouble sleeping, falling asleep, or staying asleep. When days are darker emotionally, I find myself lethargic and spending even more time than usual in bed. I've also experienced chronic insomnia just to make sure I cover all my bases. The third hallmark sign of depression is a lack of interest in normal activities and a sense of hopelessness. That has also been a reality for me at times.

The counsellor challenged me to assess if I am sad or depressed when various circumstances arise. I will say that there can still definitely be times when symptoms from each of those three categories are present. Even though I'm happily medicated, I still experience times when I'm overwhelmed, discouraged, or not feeling hopeful things will change for the better. These episodes remind me to respect that clinical depression will always be in the background. It isn't perfectly controlled by medication, and circumstances can definitely affect my mood while depression starts to again show itself to be real. I'm grateful these times are few and far between, but it's important to be aware that these feelings can surface and to be sure to talk through them with Kevin, a friend, a therapist, or all three. And at times I behave like a "normal" person and experience sadness for reasons other than my clinical depression. It's good to name emotions accurately—saying I am sad about something is drastically different from revealing that I'm feeling depressed about it. Because if depression is resurfacing in significant ways, it'll need to be addressed differently.

Despondency creeps up more easily when thrown a curve ball by MS or when in a spiral of migraines I can't seem to get under control. The next invisible illness I will discuss, IBS, can also get me down when I'm experiencing flare-ups. I conclude that I am clinically depressed, have experienced a greater level of stability when medicated, but am not immune to an extra helping of depressive thoughts when circumstances become extreme.

The title of this chapter is "It's All Right to Cry" because, well, I've done my share of crying at the hands of this illness. Kamara kept telling me that crying is acceptable, and now I feel the crying is at a more acceptable level. "It's All Right to Cry" is a song by Roosevelt "Rosey" Grier. It was one of the tracks on the album *Free to Be You and Me*, which is a collection of positive sketches and songs for children. This was a favourite record in our family when I was growing up.

Takeaways

- Mental illness should not be a taboo subject. Talking about it is acceptable and can be extremely healthy.
- Mental and emotional struggles are as important as physical ones. Don't downplay the effect your mood has on you.
- Seek help and do so before you're in desperate circumstances.
- Depression can be situational or clinical. They are both real and important, and they both require care.
- There isn't only one way to experience depression. It can involve a number of symptoms, including irritability and weepiness.
- Consider what tools (e.g. medication, talk therapy) are available to you and use the ones that are the best fit.
- When interacting with someone experiencing depression, be a listener and not an advice-giver. Questions like *Have you tried going for a walk?* are probably well-meaning, but your suggestion might not be well-received. Although the person struggling may want to go for a walk, they may not be in any shape mentally to do so.

Eight
BLAND

When my potatoes aren't salty enough, I might refer to them as bland. That would be a typical use of the word. Our nephew has been using it in droller ways. He's a teenager, so it's possible he's been influenced by today's culture and didn't actually invent these new usages. However, I like to believe he's going to be responsible for bland going viral.

His mom—Little Sister to me—started using bland in conversation with me, and now Claire and I incorporate it frequently in our own dialogue. Here are some examples of how bland might appear in our conversation:

- I got COVID. It's so bland. / *That is super bland.*
- I'm stuck waiting for a train. / *Sorry, dude. That's bland.*
- My group members are leaving me to do all the work. / *They sound really bland.*

From these examples, you might infer that the word means awkward, annoying, or uncomfortable. Basically, bland equals undesirable. I think IBS is awkward, annoying, uncomfortable, and undesirable. In a word, IBS is *bland*.

Getting Diagnosed
When my concerns with my bowels heightened, my family doctor referred me to a gastroenterologist. This specialist ordered a sigmoidoscopy, which didn't reveal anything of concern. Given the unremarkable scope and after listening to me give a complete history of my experiences in the number two department, the gastroenterologist diagnosed me with IBS-M.

There are three types of irritable bowel syndrome:
1. IBS-D: tendency toward diarrhea.
2. IBS-C: tendency toward constipation.
3. IBS-M: mixed bowel habits.

Although I have trended toward having slower bowels, I have experienced both ends of the IBS spectrum. As a result, my condition is classified as IBS-M. She recommended a low FODMAP diet, which I discuss later.

Probiotics

Some research suggests that probiotics can be beneficial for IBS sufferers. I tried using a probiotic supplement years ago, as I had heard that these supplements could be helpful for headache sufferers. I stopped taking them when I associated a drop in blood pressure with the onset of taking this supplement. I eat yogurt regularly and used to also drink water kefir, which is a slightly fermented beverage with a high probiotic count. It's similar to kombucha, but unlike kombucha, it contains no tea.

After years of drinking water kefir, I read on the ever-reliable internet that fermented foods can sometimes be a migraine trigger. I ceased drinking it, and within a week saw an improvement in my headache situation. Fermented foods are only a trigger for some people, and I didn't do a double-blind controlled study. I had almost two weeks without significant *brain pain* before we started having many rainy and stormy days, which led to what I assume were weather-triggered headaches. Health can be quite the guessing game at times! Is it the kefir? Is it the weather? Is it stress? Is it random? My bowels and head both seem to like to surprise me with what appears to be an illogical timing of symptoms.

Low FODMAP

A low FODMAP diet is recommended for IBS patients. Oops, I may have just lied to you. I had my dietician, Jessica Penner, read this chapter, and she made the following comment:

> This is one technicality that is often misunderstood, or rather misrecommended. The recommendation is to trial a low FODMAP elimination diet and, if improvement results, to test each FODMAP individually as most people are not sensitive to all types, or are sensitive at varying degrees. This re-introduction phase is super helpful for long-term adherence for most people!

The MONASH University in Australia is a leader in research in IBS and the low FODMAP diet. They put out an excellent app, which was worth the price tag. This app is educational and has an extensive database of food, detailing what makes each one naughty or nice according to low FODMAP standards.

Probably much to Jessica's chagrin, I haven't dedicated myself to trialling a low FODMAP elimination diet. My biggest obstacle is that I feel I haven't gotten to a place where my symptoms are stable. I know I do better when I follow the low FODMAP diet and worse when I deviate from it. I suppose I'm fearful of doing even worse than my baseline if I were to reintroduce certain foods to test my tolerance of them.

When I started adhering to the diet, it meant cutting out a lot of food, including gluten. I was fortunate to have already been educated about gluten-free cooking and baking, as I have three first-degree relatives with celiac disease. After a few weeks of eating gluten-free, I consumed a wheat-containing bun and did not enjoy the consequences. It was clear that I would end up being one of those pretentious hipsters, ordering from the gluten-free menu from now on.

The low FODMAP diet is quite restrictive. When I studied the list of all the foods I could no longer have, I felt overwhelmed and discouraged. However, when I looked at what I *could* eat, my spirits lifted, as I realized that there were still many foods I enjoy that weren't on the restricted and forbidden lists. This mentality is in the spirit of approaching life with an optimistic, glass half-full outlook. Focus on what you *can* do, not on what you *cannot*.

> *Focus on what you can do, not on what you cannot.*

Onions and garlic are two of the naughtiest foods, and another reason to give the title "Bland" to this chapter. There is no substitute for garlic, but I'm "allowed" to eat the green parts of green onions and leeks. It's possible to make garlic- or onion-infused oil, but it feels like rather a big ordeal to execute. I have enough on my plate (pardon the pun) without adding making oil infusions to the list. My food isn't entirely without flavour. I do enjoy the onion flavour from the approved parts of members of the onion family, and there are seasonings we use to add to the tastiness of our food. Furthermore, after being without garlic for so long, I've developed an aversion to the smell of it. Oh, and don't worry—Kevin and Claire enjoy foods beyond the limits of the low FODMAP diet; I don't insist that they deprive themselves in solidarity.

Eating Out

The result of having IBS and seeking to manage it is that I have become an extremely high-need diner. Most places can reasonably accommodate gluten-free requests, but onion- and garlic-free? Awkward. It's easier to "trust" a restaurant to accommodate my dietary needs than a well-meaning acquaintance who wants to host us for a meal. The majority of restaurants are now familiar with how to cater to people with allergies and intolerances. However, in their effort to make sure I get a safe meal, I'm usually served an unseasoned piece of meat and a baked potato, which besides garlic-mashed potatoes is my least favourite of the spud preparations.

My family and friends go to extensive measures to make sure they serve me food I can eat. However, my needs are so specific that I often opt to bring my own food for my safety and my host's convenience. The scenario that makes me the most apprehensive is spontaneously going to someone's house whom I don't know well and who will likely not be prepared for my dining needs.

A lot of people initiate a gluten-free diet because it seems to be a healthy and trendy diet. I disagree. I wish I could eat wheat again! Whole wheat has great fibre in it, and I miss how easy it used to be to increase fibre in my diet. I also miss being carefree. It can be tiring to manage the diet. However, it's 100 per cent worth it. When I stray from the guidelines, my body notices, and the discomfort and implications of an IBS flare-up are not worth the "cheating."

With all the precautions I've taken and accommodations I've made for this syndrome, you'd think I would never have IBS symptoms. Sadly, that isn't the case. IBS can still be triggered by stress or, seemingly, for no reason at all.

Gastroenterologist

For a while, I sensed I should probably see a gastroenterologist. I put off asking for a referral because I was terrified of a colonoscopy. I've heard horror stories from people who found the preparation required for the scope to be overwhelming and ghastly. I must have abnormally sensitive taste buds, because I'm an extremely picky eater despite many attempts to grow up and fall in love with vegetables. I didn't see how I would possibly be able to consume the nasty drink I'd heard so much about.

I finally got over my fear and asked my family doctor to make the necessary referral. I appreciated and connected well with the doctor who took my case. He gave me insight into my condition and concluded that most of my issues are constipation-related. And frankly, the constipation associated with this condition has seen me disappearing into the bathroom for an inordinate amount of time. I'm glad this aspect of IBS is invisible to others; bathroom matters are real, but there's a reason why they are a private affair.

He had a three-step plan of interventions I could test. As I left the appointment, I told him that I had feared he would order a colonoscopy. He responded with the most welcome words: "I don't think you need a colonoscopy." Music to my ears—someone should write a song by that name! I felt lighter in my spirit when I left the appointment, and I think I had some improvement just from being less stressed. There is exceptional value in having a professional explain what's happening and present optimistic and feasible solutions. I experienced further progress as I started implementing his recommendations.

Smart, Professional Help

Before I saw the gastroenterologist, one of the biggest helps to me had been seeing Jessica Penner, the registered dietician I quoted earlier. She's a wealth of knowledge, and I greatly benefited from hiring a professional who looked at all of my health concerns as well as lifestyle considerations. When I met with her after emailing her details of my health history and three-day food journal, I was expecting her to weigh in mainly on IBS. However, she also made recommendations to help with low hemoglobin, MS, and migraines.

A few years after I saw Jessica for the first time, I began developing slightly different symptoms. I made another appointment with her, and she was able to make many recommendations based on the report of my recent experience coupled with the extensive research she'd done before our meeting. In less than a week, I noticed an improvement in the symptoms that concerned me most, just by making a few simple changes.

One of the topics she studied was neurogenic bowel dysfunction. She explained that some of my symptoms may actually be due to what's going on with my nervous system; not everything bothering me is necessarily related to IBS. And she was onto something—the gastroenterologist confirmed that there is likely an MS component at play.

You can check out her website at www.smartnutrition.ca. There you'll find many healthy and free recipes along with an array of other resources. The woman behind Smart Nutrition is indeed a smart one! IBS might be bland, but Jessica definitely is not.

One of the reasons I appreciate working with Jessica is her down-to-earth nature. Sometimes we related in the way of her assuming a counsellor role, asking me key questions to get a full picture. As we went through my answers and worked through her recommendations, she was able to put me completely at ease, even to the point where I was comfortable talking about the most personal health details. And she has certainly understood the value in well-timed moments of laughter.

Takeaways

- Probiotics and cultured and fermented foods have health benefits for most people's bodies.
- Focus on what you *can* do, not on what you *cannot*. In other words, be positive and think about and pursue what is good in your life and good for you.
- If you're having someone over with food intolerances, be up front with them about what you're serving. Be prepared to show them an ingredient list of any commercially made products so that they can scan the ingredients and decide for themselves if they'll eat what has been prepared.
- Remember all the sneaky ways cross-contamination may happen. Did you handle peanut butter and then cook or bake without washing your hands? Does your family "double-dip" in mayonnaise when spreading it on wheat products?
- Seek professional guidance. Gastroenterologists and registered dieticians are experts when it comes to digestion.
- Write out a list of questions and concerns and take that sheet to your medical appointments. It focuses the appointment and makes sure no concerns are forgotten.

PART TWO
Living with Hope: Persistently Persevering

PART TWO

Nine
IT'S ALL RIGHT TO LAUGH

Anyone who knows me well is familiar with my dry and often sarcastic sense of humour. I keep encountering new and sometimes strange symptoms and realities. Humour has been an excellent way for me to process much of what's been imposed on me. Often the laughter comes in retrospect; sometimes it's found instantly. And whenever the giggles surface, my focus has a way of being redirected from difficulties and bleakness to optimism and levity. My new outlook makes me feel hopeful.

When using humour, it's always important to know your audience. If you're laughing at a person with a disability or someone struggling with an illness, making wisecracks at their expense would be wildly inappropriate. The "sick" person should be the one to take the lead on joking about the subject. Before you join in on that fun, make sure you're in a good relationship with them. You might find you eventually become part of the inner circle of this patient and are granted special permission to poke a little fun. As a rule, jokes should be directed at the "problem" and never at the person.

I will illustrate this with some examples, broken down into some illness-specific opportunities my family and I have found humour in.

1. Chronic migraine: I affectionately refer to my headache pain as *brain pain*. Sometimes I'll announce my condition by simply telling my family that *brain pain* is high today. This may not be the funniest way one could refer to headaches (if you have a better option, please let me know!), but I thought calling it *brain pain* was cute with the pair of rhyming words. I suppose referring to my aching with a small dose of poetry is my way of finding a bit of humour at times that don't feel amusing at all.

    Using my Cefaly device also leads to some interesting language. Claire thinks I look like I've come from outer space with an electronic gizmo magnetized to my forehead. She likes to refer to me as her alien mother. And when I start a Cefaly session, I don't announce it by saying,

"I'm going to go use the Cefaly now." I tell my family that if they're looking for me, I'll be *Cefalating*.

When *brain pain* is really high, I might give my headache a compliment. I've been heard saying, "Wow. This pain is impressive. Like it's really going all out. If pain got prizes, I bet this one would podium!" I have yet to award a gold medal for my head pain, though.

2. MS: Claire loved playing soccer as a child. For one game, her team was assigned to the field located far from the parking lot. This was a challenge because, at that time, I was experiencing a motor relapse, and my right leg was weak. I was determined to not let my nervous system be a distraction to Claire. She ran ahead and found her team warming up while Kevin ambled slowly with me to the place where we settled into our lawn chairs with the other parents. It was a big effort to get to the field; I knew that making it back to the car would be even more work because I'd be starting at a deficit. I strategically started this walk before the game ended because I knew I'd need more time.

When we arrived home, Claire walked in the door and looked back at her mom, who was panting at the top of the front steps. When I got to the door, she asked if there was anything she could do to help. "Yes," I replied. "Could you lift my leg into the house?" The threshold seemed to be Mount Everest and a mountain my bum leg was not prepared to climb. She easily and happily obliged, and I was safe and sound at home after a delightful but exhausting evening. Our whole family laughed about my request to have my leg lifted into the house. We giggled when this happened but even more so as we looked back on the event.

The hit my balance has taken since getting MS is an easy opportunity to find humour. I walk around touching walls or counters to help me find my equilibrium and feel grounded. When I don't have a sturdy point of reference, I inadvertently come up with creative dance moves. If I feel myself losing my balance, I do my best to recover with some fancy movements. Claire is usually my biggest admirer of these antics and will often imitate them in the most supportive, well-received way. She understands laughing *at* the problem and *with* the person.

My favourite humorous MS anecdote is the one I shared in the "Rollercoaster" chapter about the time I had diplopia. Claire asked to kiss me on the other head (she meant cheek), and I responded to her with, "*You're the one with two heads!*"

3. Depression: Mental illness is no laughing matter, and any humour I find in my clinical depression is almost always found in hindsight. In "It's All Right to Cry," I relayed the story of me calling the police with concern about my "missing husband" and then discovering I could still cry while medicated for depression. Looking back, we chuckle at the whole episode. Now we enjoy our iPhones, and we always make our phones available to be tracked by each other. It saves a lot of guesswork.

   Referring to my antidepressant as my happy pill and joking about its alleged instant cure was also a light moment for our family. The incongruous crying felt far from funny at the time. However, I sometimes relay to others what I was going through, and many have laughed with me when I tell them about crying just because Claire gained possession of the basketball during a game. I can understand how ridiculous it sounds, but it was troubling and felt embarrassing when it happened. I'm glad I'm laughing and not crying about it now. I'm not minimizing what that middle-aged woman in the gymnasium was going through, though. Feelings of instability are no joke.
4. IBS: I've joked with Claire that one day she'll end up in therapy, telling her counsellor about how her mom wasn't around because she was always in the bathroom. Claire has assured me that if she ends up in therapy that should be the least of my concerns. Basically, bathroom problems are just bland.

Caution

It's a massive challenge for me to go through life without laughter. If strange things happen to me and I can laugh about it, I'm convinced it's healthy to do so. I should note that joking around to avoid pain is different and something I endeavour to steer clear of. Sometimes having a tendency to joke about situations can get me into trouble. When I was in labour with Claire and the contractions were becoming increasingly intense, a medical professional asked if I should consider an epidural. Another person piped up, "Oh no, she's fine! She's still cracking jokes!" At that point, I think Kevin said, "You don't know my wife. She does this all the time, even when she's in pain." He would know—he's seen me survive many intense headaches. And I got an epidural.

My People Get It

There are certain people I can take poking fun at my challenges. Family members can joke as much as they want. They've all been with me and supported me through thick and thin, and they understand when and about what some humour is welcome. Sometimes Little Sister and I have rapid-fire text exchanges. This is one we had after she gave me feedback on the excerpt about my so-called missing husband:

> Me: Thanks for reading my excerpt. There should be a TV show called *Irrational Wives*.
>
> LS: You're a good writer. Relatable. Except I don't have MS. I hope.
>
> Me: You don't. That would be bland.
>
> LS: Yeah. You're no poster child for it. <LOL emoji> Too much?
>
> Me: Not at all. I'm thinking about making a chapter called "It's All Right to Laugh."
>
> Kevin and Claire might go to a self-defence class sponsored by Kevin's industry. The description said anyone could benefit regardless of physical strength. So I asked if I could go. Kevin replied, "No. You're a lost cause. We'll just protect you." These are facts. Also, I'm home 99% of the time.

Some might think Kevin and Little Sister crossed a line, but they knew the person they're joking with. They both read the situations right, and I received their comments well and with humour. It makes me feel more loved when people can laugh with me than when they pity me.

My niece earned the honour of performing a flute concerto, accompanied by an orchestra. I was able to attend, but it was a whirlwind day filled with activity. It was a wonderful and magical time, tremendously tiring, and absolutely worth it. While we watched my niece getting pictures taken, I was with her high school choral teacher, who came out to support her. She's also a friend of mine and someone with a similar sense of humour. I was tired and having some trouble with my balance and probably made a joke about feeling wobbly. A week later, I was slowly ascending the stairs at church. She passed me on her way up the staircase and then looked back to say, "A little slow today, eh, Robyn?" I laughed immediately. She had shown care and concern for me on the day of the concert, but she didn't express pity.

I honestly felt thankful for her playful observation. Whenever I walk up a set of stairs, it's always done slowly and deliberately, and I feel as if my obvious disability is the elephant in the room. Everyone is courteous, and usually no one says anything. It was getting to the point where I started wondering, *Am I*

NINE: IT'S ALL RIGHT TO LAUGH

climbing these stairs as fast as everyone else? No. That's impossible. They're all passing me, and I'm the only one clutching the bannister. Is everyone just walking politely past me thinking, "Poor Robyn. Look how bad her MS has gotten. She struggles so much"? *Even worse, what if they talk about me like that with others?*

I'm not suggesting people should start making such remarks to just anyone. As I mentioned earlier—you have to know your audience. My friends and family are aware of what I can take and how to dish it out in a way we can laugh at. I want to emphasize that this is *me* with *my* friends and family. Not all people living with disabilities or illness will feel this way. When I ascend stairs at a snail's pace, would I want comments from every witness? No. If you aren't sure if you're one of those people, you probably aren't.

I'm well aware of my disability, and I know it must be apparent to others. Pretending I'm not disabled or expressing pity and sadness for me are both unhelpful. I want to be seen as a person, as Robyn, but I don't need people to pretend my reality is different than I know it is.

I seriously hope you find moments to laugh while you read this book. You have my blessing! Sometimes laughter is a way to put things in perspective and reminds us not to take our circumstances too sincerely, including when we face challenges—even ones that result in the use of assistive devices. We all encounter people whose disability is made evident by their use of such tools, and it's good to know how to react. The following chapter details my experience with various assistive devices.

> *Pretending I'm not disabled or expressing pity and sadness for me are both unhelpful. I want to be seen as a person, as Robyn, but I don't need people to pretend my reality is different than I know it is.*

Takeaways

- Laughter is indeed great medicine. I don't know if I would say it's the best medicine, but it has a welcome place.
- Allow yourself to find humour even in difficulty, but never poke fun at someone else or their troubles.
- If someone makes a joke at their illness or disability's expense, it's probably okay to laugh with them. Just don't initiate the kidding around.
- Let the people close to you know how you're doing. Loved ones don't want to be in the dark about your health. Using a pain scale can be a helpful way to quickly give a "status update."

Ten
#BABESWITHMOBILITYAIDS

Years ago, I remember seeing a series of commercials on TV that highlighted some challenges people with MS face. I assume these were put out by what was then called the *MS Society of Canada*. Each of the ads followed a similar pattern. They all started with a man or woman at home and unable to perform an activity of daily living. Sometimes the children of the people with MS were shown, clearly impacted by the effect the disease was having on their parent. There was always a sombre mood, and each commercial ended with a voice-over dramatically announcing, "MS. Lives. Here." Seeing those commercials and being generally quite ignorant about the disease, I came to the conclusion that MS was completely debilitating and would be devastating to live with.

A common theme in many of the portrayals of MS was the presence of a wheelchair, scooter, or cane—and sometimes a combination of these. The people in my parents' generation with MS generally had trouble with mobility and used assistive technology such as wheelchairs. I'm sure it must have been hard for my parents when I was diagnosed to have that as their background when thinking about MS and how it was likely to impact me. At the time of my diagnosis, we were all ignorant of the many advances in treating MS and the presence of disease-modifying therapies that were being shown to lessen the impact of the disease. We didn't know how much was out there to help us feel hopeful and positive.

A Note about Language and the Hip Hashtag
I came across the hashtag #BabesWithMobilityAids when posting a picture of my rollator (more on her later). I included #byACRE in my post, which referenced the brand name of my rollator. When I followed the byACRE hashtag, I discovered many other posts featuring the same one I use. I saw young-to-middle-aged women proudly sharing something of their lives as they were enhanced by their own rollator. Some of these posts used the hashtag #BabesWithMobilityAids.

The term *babe* can refer to an attractive woman. Some may find the use of the term derogatory. When looking at the social media posts with #BabesWithMobilityAids, the hashtag grabbed my attention, and, if anything, I found the term *babe* to be uplifting and light-hearted. The pictures all showed women who were clearly disabled, evidenced by the presence of assistive devices. It sent a message that women can still be beautiful even with accessibility equipment visible. I was also inspired by examples of women with the same rollator model I use who aren't in the typical walker demographic. Disability happens at all ages.

Perhaps you were offended by the use of the word *babes*. Hopefully the preceding paragraph provides clarity on how I view the term. You may also have been troubled when you read *mobility aids*. As I learned from kind Andrew-the-Orthotist, terminology in this area continues to evolve. The term *assistive devices* is now preferred over *aids* or *mobility aids*. Please forgive me in advance for using *assistive devices* interchangeably with *mobility aids*. Now that I've been enlightened, I will incorporate the term *assistive devices* into my speech and writing, but at times I'll continue to use the term *mobility aids*; it doesn't offend me and describes the function of my rollator or scooter: these tools literally *aid* me in being *mobile*. Also, "babes-with-mobility-aids" just rolls off the tongue better than "females-with-assistive-devices."

Stigma

It took a long time for me to even consider using assistive devices, and much longer to finally embrace them. I definitely felt a stigma attached to using mobility aids and embarrassment at the notion of being seen with one. I thought more about what others would think about me than the doors that would open for me if I could accept a different reality. I certainly never imagined I would ever proudly and happily post a picture of myself with a walker or scooter on social media with #BabesWithMobilityAids. But I feel hopeful when I have the assistance I need and can participate in activities more fully.

> *I thought more about what others would think about me than the doors that would open for me if I could accept a different reality.*

My use of and comfort with assistive devices increased gradually. My late father-in-law, John, purchased a used mobility scooter for his brother. In the end, his brother didn't use it, but many of our temporarily injured family members did. I'm not sure I would have fully benefited from using the scooter when John offered it to me, but my pride didn't allow me to consider the idea. As far as I was concerned, scooters were for the elderly and infirm. I didn't see myself in either category. I would be sad to think I looked down on a "young" person who used scooters or other assistive devices. But with the stigma I associated with assistive-device-use, it's hard to believe I didn't have some feeling of superiority about my ability to function without such help.

AFOs

The first device I used to help me with walking was an AFO, or ankle-foot orthosis. Orthoses are different from orthotics, which have become common. Orthoses are often custom made and can be prescribed for a number of different challenges faced by patients. I use my AFO for assistance with overcoming the difficulties I face due to foot drop.

Baby steps. I acquired my first AFO at the end of 2018. I was initially introduced to this design when I met with the physiotherapist who works with patients of the MS clinic. She placed a leather strap around my ankle, which was secured with Velcro. Then she put metal hooks in two of the loops for the shoelaces and extended a strong piece of elastic to those hooks. Once it was in place and I started walking, my eyes lit up. I was hooked—hooked on walking without tripping.

The next step (Oh, look, another pun!) was having a prescription sent to an orthotist for the AFO. *Excuse me, Robyn, did you mean to say podiatrist or orthopedic something? No one has ever heard of an orthotist.* We are both correct. I did mean *orthotist*, and probably the majority of people have never heard of this profession. Orthotists make custom orthotics as well as a variety of braces to address challenges people face—everything from infant cranial remoulding helmets to AFOs.

I made an appointment with Andrew McPhail, who has been my outstanding orthotist for a number years. He is skilled, intelligent, and also incredibly kind. He's a master at his work and in making me feel like a person and not a patient. I'm thankful to have benefited from many different practitioners who treat me with dignity, and Andrew is a shining example of this.

Andrew has set me up with three different styles of AFOs since I met him. The first one was similar to the one I tried at my physiotherapy appointment. It worked so well that I remember feeling that my foot drop was cured while I was using it. This AFO was discreet and was, therefore, an excellent introduction to assistive devices, since I was concerned about such helps being conspicuous.

Next steps. As wonderful as this first AFO was, there came a time when my foot drop required something more powerful. My next appointment with Andrew was somewhat sobering. I was hoping a simple adjustment could be made to the AFO I already had, but a stronger elastic piece wasn't the answer. In fact, it would be hard to imagine stronger elastic than the one that came with my first AFO. The second and third iterations better addressed my increasing need for support for my foot drop. However, they would be conspicuous and probably attract questions. When Andrew showed me the direction things were headed, it took me a moment to acknowledge and accept that this would be the right move to keep me moving.

Daytime. There are daytime and nighttime AFOs. The daytime label reflects being used for activities when someone is out and about, living their out-of-the-house life. Nighttime refers to AFOs put on when the user returns home for the "night." For me, daytime just means I wear it with my outdoor shoes when I'm out, and nighttime indicates it's being worn inside, usually at my home.

My daytime braces are custom-made for me based on a cast or digital scan of my leg and foot. These orthoses have a piece of plastic that runs under the foot and behind the heel. A second plastic piece sits behind the bottom half of the lower leg. The two pieces are screwed together with a rigid joint. There's a small amount of flex in the joint, and when the straps on the lower leg portion are securely fastened, the foot is held in a somewhat flexed position. I consulted Andrew, and he let me in on the technical terminology used in his field:

> The joint is a dorsiflexion assist joint. Dorsiflexion is the ankle motion that lifts the front of the foot—toes toward nose. The main function of the orthoses I have made for you is to dorsiflex your foot through the "swing phase" of each step.

In order to use this AFO, it needs to be inserted into a shoe after the insole is removed. This means I end up wearing shoes indoors as well as outdoors. I'm able to walk without shoes and without the AFO, but if I do so too much in a day, I end up with sore leg muscles; I'm also much more likely to trip without the help of the AFO to encourage my foot to "believe in itself."

I have coverage with my provincial health program to have a new AFO made for me every two years. When it came time for my third daytime AFO, Andrew added a plantar flexion stop. This feature prevents plantar flexion while allowing dorsiflexion. In other words, it doesn't allow my foot to flex such that my toes move down (away from my nose) but does let me move my toes up (toward my nose)—well, as much as my nerves will permit.

Nighttime. At one point, Andrew proposed a nighttime AFO to address concerns I had about my feet overheating due to wearing socks and shoes all the time. This brace differed from what I'd been using, as it wouldn't slip into the footwear I already have—in fact, the hope was to avoid shoes completely while using it. My feet become hot and uncomfortable when wearing shoes so much of the time. To Claire's dismay, I will regularly announce in frustration that I have sweaty feet. She usually groans, and then to make matters worse, I start singing a "Sweaty Feet" version of Phoebe's "Smelly Cat" from the sitcom *Friends*. In frustration from my hot and uncomfortable feet, I'd often walk around the house without wearing shoes and, therefore, without my AFO.

There are two key differences in the designs of the daytime and nighttime AFOs. The first distinction is that the nighttime version has a third strap, which is added to hold the toes down. This isn't required with the daytime AFO because the user's shoes take care of that. If the toes are left to their own devices while wearing a nighttime AFO, a gap might form between the toes and the end of the brace, making it much easier for the AFO to get caught or for the user to trip. The other difference is how the sole is made. The sole on the nighttime one is made for direct contact with the floor, whereas the daytime brace would actually be slippery to walk on if not in a shoe.

AFO fashion. You've probably seen people with prosthetic limbs in a variety of colours and patterns, and orthoses have similar options. I wasn't exactly adventurous the first time I chose the look I wanted. I ended up debating between black and beige. Black would work well with my winter wardrobe with darker clothes. But I reasoned getting something that would blend in with my leg would make more sense—the beige colour would be irrelevant in winter because it would be concealed by my pant leg, but it would be a good option for when I wore shorts in summer. I was able to see samples of the options before I made my choice, but in my attempt to be less conspicuous about my AFO, I ended up choosing what I call "poor-version-of-white-people-skin-tone."

Aside: Did you know the name of a person who makes and fits prostheses is a prosthetist? A prosthetist is a sister occupation to an orthotist. The former work with artificial limbs or partial limbs, and the latter work with bracing.

I appreciate when people have fun with orthotic and prosthetic fashion. Seeing a man with a camouflage pattern on his leg prosthetic inspired me to be more daring with design in the future. The next pattern I chose is called *Ice Age*, and it features swirls of different shades of blue and grey tones. I was no longer feeling self-conscious about these more visible AFOs and proudly pointed out my new flashier one to others. My third daytime AFO is my formal attire one with an understated black and charcoal design. For my nighttime AFOs, I have one with a zebra pattern (which my cat-loving piano student relabeled as "white tiger") and one with a giraffe print.

Mobility Scooter

Unfortunately, my father-in-law never did see me accept and use the gift of his mobility scooter, as he passed away in March 2018. Later that year, our family got a puppy named Roxie. Throughout the spring, summer, and fall of 2018, Kevin, Claire, and I all enjoyed taking her for walks, often as a family. By the fall, I was noticing that walking had become more challenging; specifically, I was walking slower and had less endurance. I found myself frequently explaining to others that I can walk, just not fast or far.

My late father-in-law used the mobility scooter occasionally, but after he passed away, it made sense for it to come to our place. I was the most likely next candidate in the Olfert family to use it, and we had room in our garage for it. In the spring of 2019, I put my pride aside and decided the scooter was a gift, as it would enable me to spend time outside while providing my puppy an avenue to exercise.

People automatically made room for Roxie and me, and using the scooter opened doors to friendly encounters we wouldn't normally have with others. Folks can be intimidated when encountering people with visible disabilities because they don't know how to act. Is there something they should do to help? Should they look away? What I like best is when people look into my face and talk to me. I often try to make the first move and initiate a greeting. I might make a joke about the size of the scooter or being a bad driver—especially if I'm trying to park or reverse into a tight spot. Or I might simply play the part of someone who is happy to meet a neighbour.

I'm glad I got over my pride and finally used the scooter. It offered opportunities beyond just taking Roxie for a walk. I've used it a few times to do some shopping at our nearby grocery store. There was a time I was able to visit a friend in need across my community, and another when I could take the scooter to a dentist appointment without needing to ask Kevin for a ride.

My favourite mobility scooter story involves a conversation Little Sister had with her husband, Julio.

Little Sister:	Hey, Julio, guess what! Robyn got a scooter.
Julio:	Ahh. Umm. No offence to Robyn, but don't you think that's unwise with her balance issues?
Little Sister:	And that's why it's a mobility scooter and not one you'd find at a skate park.

Transport Chair

Somehow using a scooter to walk my little dog in my little neighbourhood didn't feel too public. Perhaps it was a soft start to using assistive devices, which scream, "The person using me is super duper disabled!" At least that was how I felt when I was worried about stigma. I actually felt no judgement or condescension from others. In June 2020, I made a more public appearance, this time with a transport chair. Claire graduated from high school that month, and I had been somewhat stressed about my ability to participate in and enjoy her graduating experience.

The biggest concern I had was how the formal pictures would happen and if it would work to include me in them. Kevin is a wonderful photographer. With our three niblings who had graduated before Claire, he spent an afternoon taking pictures of them and their friends and family on the grounds of our provincial legislature. I went along and helped out with the photo shoot for the first one, but by the time the next two graduated, I wouldn't have fared well with all the walking required, not to mention the inevitable heat in Winnipeg on a June afternoon. How would I cope with all those barriers? Would Claire have beautiful pictures taken with everyone except her mom?

Did you catch the part about Claire graduating in June 2020? You may remember the small pandemic we had that year. It quickly became apparent that *Grad 2020* was going to be a different ballgame than graduations of the past. Although there were numerous hardships associated with the arrival of COVID-19, it provided many solutions to problems I had anticipated.

Graduates were given access to their caps and gowns before they wore them to the modified ceremonies. We were able to have an afternoon of photos with Claire and a close friend of hers from another school. We met at the legislative building with this friend, her parents, and two of Claire's cousins.

Two problematic dynamics presented themselves: 1) The grounds of the Legislature are uneven and cover a large area, and 2) it was a typical warm June afternoon. We had inherited a transport chair that was used by my father-in-law in his last days, and I used this to facilitate my participation and management of the day.

A transport chair is a wheelchair with small wheels that the user doesn't maneuver themself. In other words, I was pushed around. I was there for the family pictures and was also able to witness Claire enjoy the experience with her friends. I felt a lot more thankful to have been able to participate in this way than I felt conspicuous because of the transport chair. I wasn't glued to the chair, as I stood for our family pictures and also walked around briefly to visit with the other parents. I found it comical to discover my chair had become the place everyone stored belongings that were becoming a nuisance to carry.

In my wildest dreams, I couldn't have imagined a graduation more suited to me. I learned that using a transport chair can be liberating and can allow me to participate in ways that would be too cumbersome or impossible otherwise. And *Grad 2020* showed me over and over to enjoy the lemonade sometimes offered by life's lemons.

I've used the transport chair for one other purpose also related to the pandemic. In 2021, we received mRNA COVID-19 vaccinations. These were done at the Convention Centre, and we decided using the transport chair would minimize stress about unknowns, such as how much walking and standing would be involved at our appointments. I can easily become anxious when faced with uncertainty. Knowing I'd be able to navigate the appointment without tiring physically gave me much peace.

At one point, there was no one ahead of us for quite a distance, so Kevin hit the gas as we zoomed quickly through a room to get to the next checkpoint. As this happened, I exclaimed, "Wheeee!" Guess what. People smiled, and no one gave me a sad look. It's perfectly acceptable to be happy and show joy while sitting in a wheelchair.

Walker/Rollator

I was clearly becoming more comfortable with assistive devices and being seen using them, because in 2022, I started thinking seriously about getting a walker. I'd been skeptical about walkers because I associated them with elderly, kyphotic people. I already have challenges with my posture, and walking with something that would cause me to be hunched over didn't appeal to me. However, I became aware of upright walkers. With these, the user walks in an upright position, which becomes automatic given the high positioning of the hand and arm rests. I found a local store that sold these walkers and drove across the city to check them out. Thankfully, I was able to rent one and try it before committing to a big purchase. I packed an enormous walker in my trunk, took it home, unpacked it with less grace than I would have hoped for, and proudly showed my family.

When you walk with an upright walker in your neighbourhood, you quickly become aware of how large it really is. Claire and I went for multiple walks with it and eventually gave it the name Wide Walter. Walter was happy to tour the community, and I felt he was safe and sturdy. He also drew a lot of attention, because most people haven't run into a walker as imposing as this one. He took up so much room on the sidewalk that Claire often ended up walking on the grass.

There were definite pros and cons with Wide Walter. I loved the upright posture it encouraged. The seat with backrest was comfortable, and it came with accessories and good storage. The cons centred on the implications of using such a formidable and heavy contraption. The weight helped it offer stability; however, it scored poorly when it came to ease of stowing it in and retrieving it from the trunk of our car. The whole process made me feel more awkward than I usually do. I can lift the 13.5 kg (23.5 lb) it weighs in at, but handling it to stow it isn't a pretty sight. Added to this is the complication that if I were to be using the walker, it would imply that I am walking and getting exercise, all of which could fatigue me and would definitely make the stowing and retrieving processes more burdensome. I would imagine needing help, and when an assistive device that is designed to give someone more independence ends up causing them to rely even more on others, feelings of dignity and independence tend to diminish. For me, I think it was just too much, too larger-than-life. It definitely added to feelings of conspicuousness. I've never seen one of these out in the wild and wonder if the usual customer is someone who uses it only at their residence and doesn't ever pack it in a car trunk to use remotely. It certainly filled up the trunk of our sedan, which would introduce another drawback. I'm sure they are exactly the right investment for the right user.

When I returned Wide Walter, I had Kevin with me. He spotted a walker that was in stark contrast to Walter. What Kevin found was the byACRE Carbon Ultralight Rollator. I've used the words *rollator* and *walker* in this discussion, as the terms can be used somewhat interchangeably. However, walkers also come in varieties that don't include rollators.

Technically, a walker has four legs without wheels at the bottom. The user lifts the walker, places it in front of them, and then steps. Accessories are available to allow the walker to slide forward rather than requiring the user to lift it. They look like skis and work well indoors. Most of us have seen walkers with tennis balls on their feet. Tennis balls reduce friction, although not as much as skis. They have an added benefit of making the bottom of the feet more visible, which provides additional assistance to users who have trouble with depth perception. These walkers are typically made of lightweight aluminum and don't have a seat. They offer stability for users with balance challenges.

Some walkers have wheels on only the two front feet. These are shockingly referred to as *two-wheeled walkers*. The benefit of this style is that it doesn't require the user to lift the walker in order to use it. Two-wheeled walkers still offer stability to the user and are also lightweight.

The third type of walker is a four-wheeled walker, also referred to as a rollator. Both Wide Walter and the byACRE Carbon Ultralight Rollator are rollators. The byACRE rollator is truly ultralight thanks to its carbon fibre frame. It weighs only 4.8 kg (10.6 lb). I can lift it easily, and its much smaller size makes placing it in or taking it out of our car's trunk a breeze. Aside from the ease of stowing it, the lightness of the rollator means I can easily lift it over a curb or even up or down a short staircase. Another feature is that the forward-facing design of the grips promotes upright posture. This was the clear winner.

With a referral from my favourite physiotherapist, Chad Klassen, and a grant from the MS Society of Canada, it was added to my mobility toolkit. It came with an organizer bag, which has doubled nicely as a purse. In fact, I frequently get compliments on my fashionable purse; those comments always make me chuckle inside, because "trendy" and "walker" are not words I associate with each other. Other accessories that are available to purchase include larger bags, a cane holder, and a backrest. I noticed that a cup holder was not offered, but perhaps that's to ensure users don't drink and roll.

A fun bonus is how stylish this rollator is. I think all the able-bodied people will want one too—in fact, my teenaged nephew spotted it in our house, walked with it a while, and appreciated how smooth it is. He also loved its appearance. He made me feel like all the cool kids are going to want one too. I had a choice of red, black, or white. Without hesitation I chose red. This rollator makes a statement, and as I told the salesperson who sold it to me, "If I'm going to be using a walker at forty-eight-years-old, I want it to look cool." She encouraged me to choose the flashiest colour offered at that time.

It's common for people with assistive devices to name them. I asked for suggestions for christening my new four-wheeled friend, and the runner-up was Big Sister's suggestion of *Red Rocket Rollator*. I liked the proposed name because it suggests great speed and also because I'm an avid alliteration admirer;

I concluded, though, that it might be on the lengthy side. Eventually, I settled on calling her *Rougie*.

Years ago, bilingual Little Sister started calling me *Rouge Gorge*, which means robin in French. The literal translation is *red throat*. Eventually the nickname evolved to just *Rouge* (red) or *Rougie*. I've used Rougie to walk in my neighbourhood, at the mall, at my niece's graduation, with Little in her neighbourhood, and also inside the house when I had COVID-19 and needed extra support. I'm so thankful for her and am elated that she's the perfect combination of appearing both futuristic and retro. If you haven't already done so, it's time you did an internet search for the byACRE Carbon Ultralight Rollator.

Atypical Helpers

Walking poles. Mary, one of the senior women at our church, is an avid walker. After a Sunday service, I saw her preparing to walk home with walking poles in hand. I asked her about them and wondered if they'd be useful for me. Mary uses the poles as part of her active lifestyle, not for support for a disability. I'm not a trendy hiker or speed walker; I need help with balance and stamina. I wanted to pursue the walking poles option, and this also seemed like a tactic to use assistive devices in an inconspicuous way, since they seem to be used by many able-bodied people.

A woman I met in pottery class owns a local cycle and ski shop with her husband. I contacted her to ask if they carry walking poles, and she found a pair of poles I could have at a reasonable price. The cost to invest was so low that I felt I had to try them. Using the poles was not intuitive for me—perhaps this is related to my lack of athleticism. It helped me to imagine cross-country skiing. I walked around my house with them to get used to them and even attempted using them on my treadmill. However, this was not the best choice; there's simply not enough room for one wobbly woman plus a set of poles. Thankfully, disaster was averted, as I aborted the mission upon realizing the incompatibility quickly. They've been a helpful addition to my toolbox, and I enjoy using them when walking outside.

Semi-recumbent bicycle. Aside from walking poles, I've used a few other tools to help me that are less conventional choices. For a while I felt uncomfortable cycling, especially when starting or stopping. It's easier to balance on a bicycle when it's in motion. However, starts and stops can be challenging for someone with balance concerns.

Not wanting to eliminate that form of exercise, in 2010 we looked into options that would help me continue cycling. The solution we opted for was a semi-recumbent bicycle. I test drove one outside a local bike shop and was pleased to discover that when the bike wasn't in motion, I could keep my feet on the ground. This meant I could have one foot on a pedal, ready to initiate my ride while still sitting on the seat. The result was a greater sense of stability during the vulnerable moments when initiating or ending a ride. I enjoyed using the bike for a while but have been hesitant to continue as balance has become even more of a challenge.

Treadmill. Semi-recumbent bicycles are used by a wide array of people, as are treadmills. My treadmill is next on my list. I use it regularly throughout the year because it offers stability (grips are always in reach if going off balance), instant return to home, and a controlled environment. For a while, I held on to the grips whenever I was walking on the treadmill. This allowed me to walk faster and for a longer duration. However, the grips aren't height-adjustable and are too high for me. After years of using the grips, and after a day in the fall of 2022 when I pushed myself to walk one mile in one session, it became apparent that my upper back was suffering from the unnatural posture created from leaning too heavily on the grips. Since then, I've been walking more without holding on and at a slower pace. I do reach out to touch one or both of the grips as a quick point of reference if I feel I'm losing my equilibrium.

The grips are one way the treadmill offers a controlled environment. Other ways it accomplishes this are by providing a prescribed temperature, a cooling fan, a flat surface with no surprise cracks or bumps, and less visual, auditory, and sensory information for my brain to process. Being outside is wonderful for meeting neighbours and enjoying fresh air, but it comes with a price for me. The sights and sounds are unpredictable and give my brain extra inputs to accommodate.

Another risk with walking outside is not anticipating my limits. Little Sister and I went for a walk with her beautiful golden retriever, and I fatigued to the point that I couldn't complete the trip back to my house. We sat for a while under a tree, enjoying each other's company with a patient pup. She told me she would always be happy to sit under a tree with me. I'm so thankful no one was embarrassed about the circumstances. After resting for a while, I had reset enough to complete the journey home. On a few other walks I didn't realize the distance or heat involved. Each time, my ability to continue the walk was over, but my walking partners were able to run ahead to their cars and come back for me. It's because of these kinds of experiences that I have lost some spontaneity and an easygoing approach to activities. I prefer to know as much as possible about an event ahead of time, so I can prepare accordingly.

Handrails and bannisters. I'd like to give a big shoutout to all the handrails and bannisters of the world! I'm including handrails and bannisters in this list of atypical mobility tools because they don't necessarily come to mind when the subject of assistive devices comes up. They are used widely by people with and without mobility challenges. However, they should be typical and mandatory—installed beside all interior and exterior staircases and ramps on both commercial and residential buildings. I depend on these supports to steady my balance as I ascend and descend stairs. When no handrail is present, I can often steady myself by leaning on a wall or the side of a building. A situation that causes fear and trembling is one in which there are stairs to a building with nothing to hold on to.

The following are my working definitions for bannisters and handrails:

Bannister: a freestanding structure consisting of a piece of wood, metal, or other material held up by spindles. Users can hold on to bannisters to make a safe ascent or descent up or down a staircase or ramp.

Handrail: consists of a piece of wood or other material mounted diagonally to a wall next to a staircase or ramp, allowing users to ascend and descend safely.

On more than one occasion, I've gotten on my hands and knees to climb a staircase to a residence. The first time this happened, I was delivering something to the home of a family I knew from church, but we weren't close friends. After I made my delivery, I asked (or perhaps it was more that I politely told) the young man who answered the door that I would need to hold on to his arm in order to walk down the stairs safely. He was quick to oblige and also apologetic for not having a bannister. The second time this happened, I was arriving at a good friend's house. I wasn't able to crawl up the stairs discreetly because she saw that I had arrived and she opened the door before I was all the way up. Of course, apologies abounded, and she was attentive in helping me down the stairs when I left.

I try not to feel embarrassed in these kinds of situations. It's obviously not my fault that I can't manage stairs independently, but my pride always takes a bit of a hit when my disability appears apparent and awkward. Thankfully, commercial buildings I've been in have been compliant with the requirement to have handrails or bannisters. They also often have elevators, which I'm not ashamed to use; however, I still often opt for stairs over elevators depending on how I'm doing on a given day or how many stairs I'd be required to climb.

If you're reading this and you represent one of the two houses I mentioned that didn't have a bannister for me, please know I love you. Writing an entire book in hopes you would feel confronted on this matter would be quite the excessive undertaking just to make a passive-aggressive statement to you. Before this happened to me, I wasn't as aware of accessibility needs as I am now.

Shopping carts? There's an assistive device I use that you probably do as well. It's the humble shopping cart. I went shopping for jeans once while Claire was at the mall for an extracurricular event. I find shopping for clothes exhausting, especially if it's for anything below the waist. Taking shoes and my AFO off-and-on is time-consuming and fatigues me, but the worst is probably changing long pants. Not only do I have to take off my shoes, but I then need to do a lot of literal leg work. My right leg isn't always a team player thanks to foot-drop-related weakness.

At this mall, I had previously made use of the mobility scooters, which were available for guests who needed them. On that particular day, there were no scooters available. I was committed to being at the mall for a while because I needed to take Claire home at a certain time. And I really wanted new jeans. I put on a brave face and walked through the mall and to my targeted store. I tried on a number of pairs of jeans and eventually settled on two pairs. After, I hobbled over to Claire at the centre of the mall and then proceeded with her to our car. She was a new driver and happy to drive, so that gave me a moment to just breathe and recover somewhat from the ordeal.

We encountered a complication, as we had planned to do some much-needed grocery shopping after. That plan was made when I thought I'd be able to use a scooter to relieve some of the exertion necessary for the outing. I can be stubborn, and apparently I felt we really needed whatever groceries were on the list that day. Claire was willing to go in by herself and get what we needed, and although I completely trusted her to accomplish this without any issues, I stubbornly accompanied her into the store. We got a cart, which I took over the driving of, and suddenly we were cruising—well, cruising for Robyn.

When we got home, Claire said to Kevin, "Daddy! You should have seen Mom! She could barely walk through the mall, but as soon as we got to the grocery store, she got a cart and was flying through the aisles!" She's a great hype person and cheerleader. She was struck by the stark contrast between when I was in the mall and when I was behind the cart.

Shopping carts have a lot going for them. They're sturdy, have wheels and usually move smoothly, have handles at a great height (which aids in good posture while walking), have a place to put your purchases, and are mainstream. There are drawbacks, though. Many are in need of adjustments to move smoothly; sometimes the user is forced to twist to get them to move straight forward, and that means more effort is required to push them. They get harder to push when the load they're carrying becomes heavy, and they'd be completely impractical to try to stow in your car's trunk. Besides not fitting in the boot, I would be unable to hoist one.

After that experience, I started to think a walker sounded like a great idea. However, I hadn't seen any with the feature I most appreciated about shopping carts—namely comfortable handle height. I thought I could probably make a ton of cash if I designed a walker that had the best features of a shopping cart and was also somehow stylish. I'd want my walker to be something I could take with me in the trunk of my car so that I could use it remotely. You may have guessed that I didn't get a new walker design patented. It was my appreciation for shopping carts that eventually led me to consider Wide Walter. I'm thankful I ended up with Rougie, though. She has the best combination of features I need most.

Husband. My favourite assistive device also happens to be a great kisser. Kevin has an amazing way of walking with me. He purposefully matches my pace and stride perfectly, and to any observer it would just appear as though two love birds were walking together in perfect synchronization. When I link elbows with him, I can easily descend a staircase. His insight into my needs, his caring, and the way he looks out for me constantly exceed my expectations.

Claire is a close second. She's had much experience observing Kevin and me, and she has become quite intuitive in identifying a need and appropriately providing assistance to me and others.

I suppose you could consider using non-traditional assistive devices a bit of a "life hack." Over the years, I've discovered many other ways to get creative and make my world more manageable. What follows in the next chapter is a discussion of skills and strategies I've used.

Takeaways

- Overcoming the thought of stigma and concern with appearances may go a long way in your enjoyment of life.
- Avoid assumptions about both others and yourself.
- A gradual introduction to something new is often in order. It can take a while to adjust mentally to a new reality. Allow yourself to grieve the loss of something you once had, but commit to making wise decisions about moving forward.
- Look at people and avoid staring at their assistive device(s). It's natural to be curious about someone's situation, and a person living with a disability would much rather people of any age ask them sincere questions over absorbing piteous stares and feeling they're being put on display.
- Make sure your home or business is outfitted with bannisters or handrails.
- If you own a business, ensure that your front door has an accessibility open/close button.

Eleven
DISABILITY AND FATIGUE HACKS

Over the years, I've adapted my systems for tackling certain tasks in an effort to manage my disability and fatigue challenges. As my limitations change, I constantly evolve how I approach various activities, and sometimes discontinue something if needed. This has taken a humble attitude, creativity, and self-awareness. The self-awareness aspect can be a tricky one.

My version of self today is different from what it was twenty years ago and what it will be in the future. I need to remember to be flexible in my approaches as my needs change. But I feel hopeful when I find creative ways to achieve my goals and can participate meaningfully in contributing to our household. I also feel hopeful when people come alongside me, providing the help I need to manage a situation. As all the influencers on YouTube say, "Let's jump right in." Divide and Conquer Splitting up large tasks into smaller ones is a strategy I adopted early in my MS illness. I first applied this to how I approached housework. I took stock of all the chores I would like completed in a given week and assigned each of them to a different day of the week. I was remarkably diligent in sticking to the routine I proposed to myself.

> *My version of self today is different from what it was twenty years ago and what it will be in the future. I need to remember to be flexible in my approaches as my needs change.*

In 2003, when I came up with my housework plan, I enthusiastically explained my new system to others. Someone remarked, "That's great and all, but don't you feel like your whole house is never clean?" My response to that was that I never felt like my whole house was ever dirty. It was a way of making an insurmountable project manageable.

Adapt and Lower Expectations
In time, I needed to make some practical and mental changes to my approach to housework. I have a love-hate relationship with showers. I appreciate their

convenience, and I do love being clean. But soap scum is the target of some less grateful thoughts. Eventually, cleaning the shower came to the point of being too overwhelming and exhausting to do in one session. The solution was having Kevin take over the task. He's our best and most thorough cleaner. He also has many responsibilities pulling him in countless directions. These realities resulted in the shower not being cleaned as often as I would like, and me feeling like a burden and a useless nag whenever I would mention that the shower was due for a cleaning. Kevin never said I was a burden, useless, or a nag, but being dependent on others has a way of playing mind games with me, as I'm prone to battling unhelpful and inaccurate thoughts on how others perceive me.

After this went on for a while, I realized I needed to do two things: 1) adapt and 2) lower expectations. I would love for the shower to get a thorough cleaning weekly. Since I wasn't willing to escalate nagging to achieve this goal through inappropriate and irritating means, I devised a plan to reassign the task to my chore list.

I knew I had to change my approach, so I made a two-step plan: 1) mentally divide the shower into sections and clean one section at the end of each shower and 2) turn the warm water off while cleaning. This second step is an obvious one, but almost as much as I dislike overheating, I'm not keen on shivering. And this is why step two ensures that step one happens; I can't bite off more than I can chew if my cleaning time is limited to the time I can tolerate being colder than I'd prefer.

Guess what. This worked flawlessly at first. In the spirit of new-goals-that-will-improve-everything, I was an enthusiastic and diligent participant in the steps to achieve this ambitious-for-me objective. The shower was cleaned at least twice in a row as per the plan. Following those two epic weeks, my energy waned. I also found myself with commitments dictating shorter showers with no time left for cleaning at the end. This led to a larger gap between shower cleans, which, of course, led to more stubborn soap scum. Whenever I stray from a new habit for too long, I find it hard to get back on track. #relatable?

Know My Limitations
I'm not a quick study when it comes to reflecting on past events to assist me in making predictions for how a current or future one will turn out. A clear example of this is the time I single-handedly mopped all the hard surface flooring on our main floor. When I got to the end, I collapsed next to my cleaning tool and announced, "The mop tried to kill me." Kevin and Claire looked at me and

said, "This is not your job anymore." But that didn't stop me from trying again months later.

Outsource

Outsourcing is both easy and difficult. It's easy in the sense that it takes tasks off *my* plate and puts them on someone else's. It's difficult because that means it takes tasks off my plate and puts them on *someone else's*. As I often struggle with misplaced guilt, I can feel badly about other people doing tasks I feel should be assigned to me. However, the reason for outsourcing something is because it has become too challenging for me. The key to success with all this is who my people are—Kevin and Claire. They both appreciate direct communication, but I tend to default to hiding my request for help amidst a long discourse about them only doing something if it works for them, if it's not too inconvenient, if it's something they're happy to do, if it fits into their schedules, and on and on I go. Kevin will sometimes stop me mid-ramble and say, "Just tell me what you want me to do." I then do my best to be clear about what I'd like without being bossy or demanding. I often apologize to Kevin for needing him to do so much for me, and he's always reassuring about being happy to help. I could never have imagined being this blessed.

Accept Help

This disability hack is in the spirit of the previous two. When I need something outsourced, I have to remember to ask for help and then receive it graciously without protest. Anticipating and knowing my limitations help me realize when it's time to seek support from others. This can extend beyond our home and involve people other than Kevin and Claire.

I've become bolder in asking for help when shopping. Twice this has meant asking for a large bag of dog food brought to and placed in my trunk. The first time this occurred, a tall, young man provided the assistance, but the next time, my help came from an employee who was even smaller than I am. It felt awkward, but she was capable of carrying my bulky and heavy purchase. I've also had a more senior woman help me out by bringing my groceries to the car. These are humbling moments, but people have always been kind and happy to offer assistance. They've never suggested I should feel silly for asking. I often preface my request with something like, "I'm a little bit disabled. Would you mind …?" But I need to stop sounding apologetic for my disability. I suppose I feel I owe my helpers an explanation, as my disability is due to reasons that might not be initially apparent.

Say "No" and Manage My Schedule

With my people-pleasing personality, I find it difficult to decline when someone makes a request of me or invites me to an event. I've been learning to say some version of the following: "Thanks so much for thinking of me and asking. I need to look out for how I use my energy, and the activity you're asking me to join sounds wonderful but probably too taxing for me at this time. I'm sure I would love participating in it if circumstances were different. I hope you'll continue to think of me when similar opportunities arise, and also continue to be understanding if it doesn't work out for me." Maybe one day I'll learn to say it all more succinctly. However, if that happened, the people who know and love me would wonder if they were really speaking to Robyn. How would you respond if someone said, "No thanks. Keep asking. I'll probably say no. You okay with that?"

I'm learning to keep a balanced and leaner schedule than I often like. Doing this requires managing how many "events" are on my calendar. Examples of events for me could include an appointment, teaching piano, going to a care group meeting, and meeting a friend for lunch.

I do best when there's only one event per day, but that's not always realistic. If there ends up being a three-event day or one that ends too late, I'll pay for it the next day. At times it's absolutely worth it to have a day that's too busy. I will happily spend the following day or days lying low, getting extra rest, and not engaging in any events if I can help it. In the "Tired of Being Tired" chapter, I talk about learning from my aunt the importance of banking my energy. If a multi-event day or weekend is coming up, I'll get more rest than I normally require, enabling me to have reserves to draw on to sustain me through the future excitement. In the end, it's about making choices and prioritizing.

Margin

Margin is a great book that addresses the concepts in the previous hack. This helpful guide was written by medical doctor Richard A. Swenson, after observing "a steady parade of exhausted, hurting people"[3] visiting him in his office and seeking his help—not for the pain of "marginless living" but for the myriad other painful reasons people seek medical care. He definitely did what he could to lessen their physical pain while he continued to note more and more examples of people who had exceeded their limits. He wrote *Margin* over a ten-year period and saw it published in 1992.

It has been over twenty-five years since I first read the book, but the concepts still resonate—concepts he began observing more than ten years prior to my

---

[3] Richard A. Swenson, M. D., *Margin* (Colorado Springs: NavPress Publishing Group, 1992), 15.

introduction to *Margin*. Swenson defines margin by explaining, "*Margin is the amount allowed beyond that which is needed.* It is something held in reserve for contingencies or unanticipated situations. Margin is the gap between rest and exhaustion, the space between breathing freely and suffocating. *It is the leeway we once had between ourselves and our limits.* Margin is the opposite of overload."[4]

Building margin into my life is a by-product of intentionally managing my schedule to create this leeway. Having space in this way makes it more likely that I'll be able to attend to concerns of high importance, which are sometimes unexpected.

Work Ahead

I adopted this hack even before I faced disability. I have memories of procrastinating in high school. My drive to achieve high marks meant I always handed my work in on time and usually to a high standard. However, the result of putting things off meant too often missing out on valuable sleep.

Kevin and I have often had different approaches in this area. When going on a trip, he would love everyone to get on board with packing well in advance. It gives him peace to know there will be no last-minute loose ends. I need to make more of an effort to facilitate this, and it would surely give me more peace as well. He also works ahead with making our breakfasts every day. He and I eat oatmeal every morning. Because we're exciting like that. Faithfully, every evening before bed, he sets out bowls with water, oats, and flax seed in them, ready to pop in the microwave the next day. This is not a middle-age crisis. Kevin is a man of consistency. In our first year of marriage, we had a conversation that went something like this:

> Kevin: What are you taking to work for your lunch tomorrow?
> Me: I don't know. I'll figure it out in the morning.
> Kevin: We can prepare your lunch now. Then you won't have to worry about it in the morning and be rushed.
> Me: Oh, but that's not how the system works. I've been doing it this way since packing lunches in junior high. The simple routine is as follows: hear alarm; look at the time; adjust the time in my head to the correct time because I set the clock ahead to trick myself into getting up earlier; given that information, calculate how many times I can press snooze; press snooze the maximum acceptable number of times; recalculate; press snooze again;

---

[4] Swenson, *Margin*, 91–92.

have a shower and dry my hair; eat breakfast; hurriedly make a sandwich and throw a couple other things in the lunch bag; rush out the door and hope to make it to school on time. It's all about the adrenaline. I haven't changed the system because somehow I haven't been late for work yet.

Kevin: <sigh>

It would make sense for me to have favoured the delayed gratification of waking up to a pre-made lunch, since I'm far from a morning person. Over time, I've grown to appreciate Kevin's ways and have adopted his saner approach more and more throughout our marriage. I started my teaching career before we got married, and I was definitely a fan of working ahead in many areas. Writing report cards and marking student work are both important tasks that can escalate in how daunting they are if not tended to in a timely manner. I was often the first teacher with completed report cards and was diligent in staying on top of correcting tests and assignments.

When I became disabled by fatigue and physical weakness, this background served me well. I learned to plan to clean the house one chore at a time, divided up among the five weekdays, as I discussed earlier. In a similar vein, when energy permitted, I peeled and chopped up carrots for the freezer for future meals.

There's another area, which is unrelated to domestic duties. Since I don't participate in cooking and cleaning as fully as I used to, what follows is a more relevant and current example: I like to make birthday cards for people. I have a list in my phone of upcoming birthdays of loved ones and prepare cards in advance. It gives me peace to know the card is already made and we'll be ready when the occasion arrives. I can't predict with any confidence how I'll be feeling when a birthday celebration rolls around. Knowing I'm prepared just in case is reassuring.

It seems that as I've gotten older, I've learned a few new tricks. Amazing. Read on to hear about tricks unrelated to disability and fatigue.

Takeaways

- Divide your tasks into manageable assignments and work to complete them.
- Accept that sometimes changes are needed and make them. This may require you to lower your expectations, and that's okay. Pobody's nerfect.
- Recognize what you're able to do and also what is out of reach.
- Kindly delegate to others.
- When you need help from others, get over your pride and accept it.
- Know when to say "no" and protect yourself to manage your schedule.
- Work some cushion into your schedule to be able to accommodate unforeseen circumstances.
- When possible, tackle obligations before they're due. Your future self will thank you, especially if your future self has encountered unexpected challenges.

Twelve
OLD DOG, NEW TRICKS

I have a quotation from C.S. Lewis on display in my piano studio. I like to tell my students that when they see the word "old" in the following quote, they can substitute "young" to fit their demographic (except I don't say demographic to young children):

> "You are never too old to set a new goal or to dream a new dream." ~ C.S. Lewis

When facing health challenges like mine, it's easy to start feeling as though you're "washed up." However, I make an active effort to stay mentally sharp and love learning new skills. I've had moderate-to-good success with many of these new pursuits, and some have seen me more or less just getting a participation certificate. But each of these valuable experiences has enriched my life, sometimes in significant ways. The big message of this section is that health challenges, disability, and age do not put an abrupt halt on a desire to learn and grow. I wouldn't go so far as to say that you can accomplish anything you set your mind to. That's misleading and is certainly not true for me. No matter how passionately I set my mind to running a marathon, I know that will never happen. But there have been other areas that have been worth focusing on. And I feel hopeful when I learn skills and grow in knowledge. It reflects my striving to have an attitude of engagement and optimism.

It Really Was All Greek to Me
I learned Koine Greek. Just kidding. I know the Greek alphabet and can fumble through pronouncing written Greek.

Once upon a time, there was a pastor at my church with a love for the original languages of the Bible. He offered free introductory courses in Greek and then Hebrew. I have a friend who studied Greek and Hebrew in seminary. I always admired how this knowledge enabled her to study the Bible in a way that seemed more in-depth. Often pastors will make reference to a Greek or Hebrew word when giving a sermon. I appreciate learning about the background of a word or phrase, as it often sheds light on something that would be missed if only reading an English translation.

When these day-time Greek classes were offered, I jumped at the opportunity to participate. I was a conscientious student, making colour-coded flashcards, and I even shared my flashcard files with my peers. I bought the recommended textbook and workbook initially but got so inspired that I eventually purchased a Greek New Testament as well. Everything was going smoothly with nouns, but I hit a snag when it came to verbs. I've always excelled when it comes to academics. However, this time it seemed I reached my cognitive limit. My memory lapses have certainly been noticeable; I'm becoming famous for having a thought one moment and then forgetting what I want to say seconds later. Kevin and Claire are kind in letting me interrupt before a thought vanishes completely. I often discover what I was once so determined to say was not as important as listening to others in the conversation.

Sometimes I will quickly interrupt whomever I am with and ask them to remember a key word. That has proven to be a helpful strategy and doesn't require a long interruption. I think the simple act of articulating the prompt out loud is often enough for me to be able to remember what I wanted to say when it would naturally be my turn to speak.

Just because I discontinued taking these classes doesn't mean I regret doing so. Even with my small exposure to Koine Greek, I still came away with more Bible study tools. I like to joke about being a Greek school dropout because it reminds me of the song, "Beauty School Dropout" from the musical *Grease*. If I dropped out of something, it means I was enrolled in it first. And that counts for trying in my books.

Not in My Wheel-House
In 2015, I acted in a way that was out of character for me when I pursued something both physical and artistic—two areas I've found challenging. The story goes back to May of that year when a dear aunt experienced a burst brain aneurysm, which resulted in a stroke. She was in a coma for months. Before this medical crisis, Auntie Jan was an accomplished potter. When September rolled around, I saw a listing for an introductory pottery class close to where we live and signed up as a way of finding a connection to my lovely aunt, for whom we had been praying in earnest.

The class I signed up for offered six weeks of handbuilding lessons followed by four weeks at the potter's wheel. During handbuilding, we tackled various projects involving shaping clay with our hands, tools, and moulds. My creative juices don't exactly flow when it comes to open-ended artistic tasks. I'm more drawn to structure and rules. This was indeed a stretch for me. I found the class strenuous because it was a strain to skip my nap and push myself to stay awake for an afternoon class. Doing something more physical than I was used to and concentrating on learning something new while in a fatigued state were burdensome. I looked forward to the time on the wheel the most, as that's what I associated with my aunt's work. People working at pottery wheels have always been intriguing to me.

At the conclusion of my introductory course, I was hooked on pottery but not on handbuilding. I was anxious to learn more about working at the wheel and found a different class that was only on "throwing pots" on the wheel. I signed up and convinced a friend of mine to join me in the class, which started in January 2016. To give you a measure of peace, nothing was literally thrown across the classroom. When the word *throwing* is used in the context of pottery, it refers to the action taken to make early pottery wheels spin. *Pots* can refer to any piece of pottery a potter is working on. Examples of some of the pots I made are bowls, plates, mugs, and casseroles. Not once did I make anything I would boil carrots in on my stovetop.

After the first class, I felt inspired and excited. After the second and third classes, I was almost ready to give up. I discovered that learning this new skill was challenging and resembled nothing you've seen in a certain Patrick Swayze movie. Eventually my skills picked up enough that I was able to produce items I was excited to eventually take home and use. However, the learning curve remained steep. The wonderful community of more seasoned students, who were always willing to offer guidance, kept me in the game. I went to my weekly classes as well as all the open practise times. There was so much camaraderie at those sessions, and they became an important social outlet.

I continued taking in all the classes and going to all practise times possible. By the end of summer, I was considering buying a wheel. To make a long story shorter, I was able to purchase a wheel my aunt used to work on. She was making improvements and went through a lot of challenging rehabilitation after she woke up from her coma. Right! I forgot to tell you that she survived. After a long ordeal of various hospitals and a rehabilitation facility, my uncle took his precious wife back home, where she continued to make improvements.

Before the stroke, she'd taught pottery classes and had a studio with many wheels. It became evident she was unlikely to return to potting (at least not to the degree she had before the stroke), and I was able to buy a wonderful wheel. Less than a year after starting this hobby, I found myself working at one of her wheels where she had spent time creating many stunning pieces. I did feel a strong connection to her and often shared pictures of my work with Auntie Jan and Uncle Randy. They gave me only positive feedback and encouragement. I so wished circumstances were different and for her to be able to teach me the techniques she'd used. They live in Kentucky, so apart from the stroke restricting these kinds of interactions, geography was also an obstacle.

Fortunately for me, Auntie Jan's youngest brother and his wife were visiting my Kentucky relatives when I first mentioned to them my interest in buying a wheel. I was looking for advice, not imagining I'd actually be able to buy one of Auntie Jan's wheels. Due to this great timing and room in Uncle Eldon and Auntie Bernice's vehicle, it was driven across the border right to my garage. Shipping a wheel internationally would have been cost-prohibitive. Do you ever feel like God is smiling down on you? It's hard to imagine timing like that being coincidental.

The wheel first found a home in our garage, where clay splashed all over Kevin's classic car. Oops. Sorry, darling. Wet clay can be rather messy. As a surprise Christmas present, at times when I was out of the house or napping, Kevin and Claire worked to make a pottery room in the basement. It was the first area to be finished on the lower level of our home. I dedicated the room to Auntie Jan and spent many hours working to become a better potter. I had successes and saw some improvements. My progress was slow, though, and I often felt discouraged.

Pottery became hard on me physically, mentally, and emotionally. Posture at the wheel is not ideal, and my neck and back didn't thank me. Recycling clay was another obstacle. When learning, and even when someone is a seasoned potter, there can be a fair bit of clay not making it into a pot to be fired. To lower both cost and waste, I pursued the process of recycling this clay, and that was a physically demanding ordeal. I felt obligated to go downstairs and work at my pottery especially because I had a great home studio with excellent equipment. I almost began to have feelings of resentment and was often frustrated that I still found the process difficult and unnatural. Eventually, my body, mind, and emotions were too tired to continue.

In 2020, I sold the wheel to a former classmate. It went to a great home, and as part of the sale price, I negotiated that the buyer would make a piece for me with her famous cartoon chickens. Rita is a true artist, drawing chickens on many of her pieces and glazing them with exquisite results. She kindly made a whimsical cookie jar for our family with her comical chickens all around it. It was hard to say goodbye to something I had invested so much time, effort, and finances in. What surprised me, though, was how much easier it was than I thought it would be. I felt relief when I closed that chapter, and looking at the cookie jar from Rita only brings smiles and giggles.

White Belt

My short pursuit of Taekwondo continues this theme of dropping something but trying hard first. In 2018, I went to watch Little Sister's middle child, Sam, at his Taekwondo class. I was intrigued, observing people of all ages working together to learn this Korean martial art. I asked Master McKenna, the black belt who was the organizer of the dojang, if they'd ever had any participants with disabilities. She said they hadn't but were warm to the idea. With that open door, I signed up to join the beginner class for ten weeks.

Taking Taekwondo was a decision not based entirely on logic or known facts about Robyn Olfert. I don't have an athletic bone or muscle in my body. I have attempted to address this in a variety of ways, all of which make me laugh now when I reflect on the incredulity of it all. I'd never been a participant in organized sports and optimistically joined my sister's water polo team, which was in need of players. I was thirteen, and the other players each had at least two more birthdays under their bathing suits. Front crawl is a must for water polo and was a weak stroke for me, but I did enjoy swimming. I went to exactly one practice and one game before throwing in the towel—a literal towel in this case.

I had also missed out on land-based sports teams so was behind on skills others had been honing. To address my lack of basketball finesse, I spent a summer afternoon on my friend's driveway in hopes of learning how to perform a layup. Despite my tutor's patience and kindness, not one swish from this skill was accomplished by me. I hadn't given up, though. Kevin's and my first date was spent with my sister and her husband in my school's gymnasium on the weekend. I had arranged for this couple to teach me skills in sports such as volleyball and basketball—that was before there were developments in my relationship with Kevin.

Eventually he and I wanted to get together without the rest of our Bible study group, and for some reason, I thought it would be wise to invite him to join us in the gym. That was the falsest of advertising there ever was—Kevin might have thought I must be a sporty gal, initiating an athletic-themed first date. Two truths were quickly revealed on that Saturday morning: 1) not sporty and 2) I was willing to be vulnerable, letting him see me make attempts at growth in an area I wasn't proud of. We were married exactly one year later, so it seems my strange advertising methods worked in the end. Phew.

Why then did I join a class for a martial art that emphasizes kicking when one of my kickers wouldn't be up for the task? Apparently, I'm always hopeful and continue to seek growth and vulnerability. I'm thankful I engaged in this illogical pursuit, though. To say I had to modify the skills would be an understatement. I didn't research Taekwondo before signing up for the classes, which is another unusual aspect in all of this, as I generally do a thorough study before incorporating something new. My scrutiny of the suitability of the new activity for me was essentially observing a class, appreciating the instructor, and admiring the interactions I saw between students and teachers.

My Taekwondo classes taught me a great deal, with many unexpected lessons. I could never say enough to celebrate the amazing community developed in the dojang. There are traditions and expectations in a Taekwondo class. The first routine I learned was that each time I entered the dojang, I was to look at the South Korean flag hanging on the wall and bow out of respect. The bowing continued, as the next order of business was to find every black belt in the room, go up to each of them, and bow to them. They would, in turn, bow to me. Expressions of mutual respect were evident throughout each class, including the way we would answer questions asked of us by the most senior black belt, who earned the title of Master. All of the other black belts were addressed by their last name preceded by the title Mr., Mrs., or Miss. I found myself addressing a sixteen-year-old girl as Miss MacDonald and sensed no air of superiority from her or any of the black belts.

Although our belt levels ranged from white belt to fourth dan black belt, representing a fourteen-level difference, we all worked together. The beginner class with white and yellow belts met separately for teaching and reinforcement of the various basic blocks, punches, and kicks. Depending on the belt or stripe we were working on, different patterns needed to be learned. In each class, we spent time as a large group at the beginning warming up together and then again at the end doing various exercises. One of the guidelines the dojang followed was that if any lower belt approached any black belt for help, the black belt would provide the requested assistance.

The black belts were always ready and willing to help with explanations, tips, and guidance on refining our skills. They weren't intimidating to approach for assistance, and they always gave me the feeling that they remembered being at the beginner levels too.

My physical challenges due to MS were known to the others, and everyone was rooting for me and without condescension. I thought I was going to learn about martial arts, and I did; however, just as notably, I learned about how this group of students and teachers, both novices and masters, became a welcoming and inclusive community that fostered learning and taking risks in the most supportive way.

I was making progress in being able to remember what to do when each skill was called by Master McKenna. I was also learning Pattern One, all in preparation for the first belt test that would see me earn a yellow stripe on the white belt I got with my dobok. Alas, before I was ever fully ready to take such a test, and before the next set of tests were held, I had to drop the class. I had another "drop out" to add to my list: Greek School Dropout, Pottery Pauser, and Taekwondo Class Quitter. Sadly, I never had the satisfaction of advancing past the white belt all beginners are given. I received a certificate saying I had completed the ten-week introductory class. In essence, it was yet another participation award, but it represented a significant amount of effort and is probably the participation certificate I'm most proud of.

I had to abandon this interesting and out-of-character pursuit because my foot drop symptoms were worsening. How fitting that the foot *drop* led to *dropping* out of something. Foot drop was not new to me at the time, but it had worsened significantly.

I have one big victory I associate with taekwondo, though. A few weeks before I enrolled in the class, I started teaching piano to two children from the same family. They didn't know I had MS until the following fall when I began wearing my second and more conspicuous AFO. When first diagnosed with MS, I had kept my diagnosis a secret for about a year until I went on medical leave from my teaching position. After the MS cat was out of the bag, it felt good to freely tell people about it, and I think I was overly forthright and even sometimes borderline dramatic when revealing I had a big, scary disease. However, eventually I longed for some anonymity and for people to know me as Robyn and not as Robyn-with-MS. This happened for me with this family, and I sincerely felt they appreciated me for my skills as a piano teacher, for my personality, and for my values. It was refreshing to have people see me without looking through the lens of feeling sorry for me due to my health, or lack thereof.

Instant Recall

At the end of 2019, I reflected back on the year and concluded that memorizing Bible verses had given me the most joy. I discovered a new love for scripture memory and the Word of God and began intentionally memorizing verses, ending the year with at least one hundred verses committed to memory. I discovered an ingenious app, simply called *Bible Memory*, that made learning new verses a much quicker process than I had imagined it would be for a middle-aged woman, especially one who had noted some cognitive setbacks.

I made it a habit to recite my verses in my head after going to bed and often turned them into prayers. It was the most beautiful way to fall asleep. Contrary to what the heading of this section might suggest, my recall wasn't always instant. I thought of using the heading "Total Recall," but that would be even further from the truth, because it might imply memory of the totality of the Bible. At the time I'm writing this section, it's been approximately four years since I began memorizing verses in earnest. I now have just over 150 verses that I review regularly. I have found that there's a limit to how many new verses I can add, and I think 150 might be where I plateau.

Found Art?

If anyone asked me if I consider myself an artist, I would emphatically deny it. However, I have found myself engaging in artsy activities of various sorts since approximately the second year of the COVID-19 pandemic. These pursuits came about quite by fluke. I find it so interesting to trace the chain of events that resulted in something of such significance in my life. Each of the following ended up being pivotal moments in my little art story:

1. My aunt, who was an accomplished potter, had a stroke and was in a coma. This led to me taking a pottery class.
2. I convinced my friend Alana to take a pottery class with me after the city class concluded. This led to Alana also getting a potter's wheel so that she could dedicate more time to the art.
3. Alana had a display at a local craft sale where I ran into Janet, a classmate from high school who was showcasing her lettering and upcycled mittens. This led to me following her social media accounts.
4. I happened to notice that Janet was doing a live workshop on brush pen lettering and tuned in to see what I could learn by trying out the techniques with the humble pencil. This led to me asking for and receiving brush pens for my birthday.

5. YouTube videos were my next teachers in learning how to use my new brush pens. This led to viewing many different lettering, traditional calligraphy, and drawing accounts.
6. One of the "creators" behind an account hosted an online workshop, featuring tutorials in various art forms. This led to inspiration to draw botanicals, watercolour, and some mixed media work.
7. I started making cards for people for various occasions, using my new skills in drawing flowers and different lettering forms. I made "pretty" cards with different flowers for a while. This developed into drawing cartoon animals with punny captions.
8. Claire worked for Hope Centre Ministries (HCM) for two summers. HCM is a disability support organization whose mandate is to provide spiritual care and belonging for people living with disabilities. I wanted to participate in their annual peer-to-peer fundraiser, and it came to my attention that they needed birthday cards to send out to their participants. This led to me participating in their fundraiser and making fifty cards one year and one hundred the next for them, and to investing in instructional drawing books and better stationery supplies.
9. I continue to pursue growth in watercolour and making punny cartoon animal cards. It's always a challenge to simply enjoy the process and be positive about my results, realizing everyone progresses at a different pace. It's evident I have indeed made progress and thoroughly enjoy the process.

Encouragement was lavished on me at every step and was a notable reason I continued down this path. Kevin and Claire are my biggest fans and are always up for my latest show-and-tell presentation. They respond with smiles, laughter, delight, and admiration. It astounds me every time I hear people telling me that I'm creative, artistic, or "so good at drawing." Guess what. I am not amazing at any of it. What I lack in raw talent, I make up for in patience, determination, and a really good and well-used eraser.

Cubing

Not too long ago, I would have never imagined being able to solve a Rubik's cube. However, I found that learning to accomplish this feat was much more accessible than I imagined. There are many systems that can be broken down and practised. I have my nephew, Sam, and Little Sister to thank for getting me started. Oh yeah, and a little app called YouTube. I started with a 3 × 3, then added the Megaminx (a dodecahedron—twelve-sided "cube"), a 4 × 4, a 5 × 5, a 2 × 2, and finally a 7 × 7. It has been an engaging and enjoyable pastime that probably looks a lot more difficult than it really is.

Calendar Calculations

This next one is another skill I thought would be out of my reach. If you tell me the month, day, and year in which you were born, in less than one minute I can tell you which day of the week your birthday fell on. Usually. I do make mistakes sometimes, especially when I'm tired or out of practice. When Little Sister told me that her son, Sam, could do this in seconds, I was in shock and awe and had to know the magician's trick. It turns out that, like solving cubes, there is no actual magic, but there was profound mystery until I hunted down a YouTube video, which explained the process.

You may have guessed that math is involved and inferred mental calculations are at work. This is true. There are also a few landmark days to remember, a code to translate numbers to days of the week, and memorizing a pattern that assigns a number to each century. It's also important to understand when leap years occur and make allowances for that at one stage. Through a combination of the YouTube video, Sam's advice, and my own practice, I've developed my own method, which I find works best for me. Let's hang out sometime—I'd love to teach you!

Geography

In keeping with the theme of Little Sister and Nephew Sam introducing me to new ways to stimulate my brain, this last example of new knowledge I acquired is no exception. At a family gathering, Little Sister appropriately #humblebragged about her son, Sam, being able to locate all the countries in the world. Come again? It turns out Little Sister could have tooted her own horn too, because she was in the same geography-knowledge boat. In fact, their whole family gets in on these things and are all bright and interesting people.

So is there a secret? Some super easy shortcut to achieve this kind of mastery? Well, there is a website and an app, and they've turned learning geography into an engaging game with a slightly addictive quality. *Seterra*[5] by *GeoGuesser* is your ticket to the best geography party in town.

There are many quizzes to choose from—from countries on one continent, to states in the US or provinces in Canada, to obscure quizzes covering the regions in Chile or districts in Suriname. You can choose from map-based quizzes as well as ones covering flags.

---

[5] "Seterra—The Ultimate Map Quiz Site," Seterra, accessed September 17, 2024, https://www.geoguessr.com/quiz/seterra.

Aside from North America, South America was the continent I was most familiar with and had fewer countries than most of the other continents. As a result, I started there and was amazed at how quickly I learned to select the location of each country in South America. I continued with areas most familiar to me and with quizzes with the fewest questions. This built my confidence and also increased the fun factor and my desire to learn even more. Success does that. Eventually, I was able to get 100 per cent on the quiz entitled "195 States Recognized by the United Nations." That surprised me. At forty-nine years old, I easily learned something I would have assumed would be too daunting of a collection of knowledge to master. It should be noted that this does take time, but not an inordinate amount. I spent time doing quizzes here and there throughout the day and didn't move on to new ones before the first ones were under my belt.

Robyn, is this something you do just to flex your geography muscles around others? Is this practically useful? I haven't heard you say you're a travel agent or geography teacher. Rest assured, it has had many benefits! For one, it's learning. It's expanding my knowledge base. I'm spending time in a wholesome activity that gives me new topics to think and talk about. Furthermore, I've had interesting conversations with others as a result of this learning. I met a lovely woman at church and found out she comes from Ghana. I lit up and asked, "Isn't Ghana close to Togo and Benin?" She enthusiastically affirmed. I like meeting new people, learning about their background, and having a possible extra point of connection. If I were on the other side of the world from the small country I refer to as "back home," and someone knew where it was without me needing to explain, I think I would feel special and want to keep our conversation going. That's just one example; I have many others. Conversations don't usually stop after we've talked about geographical positions. It's a great starting point, though.

This feels like quite the "toot my own horn" kind of chapter. I hesitated to include it, but I did want to demonstrate that people with disabilities and illnesses are not all washed up. Our interests and strengths may be evident in surprising ways, but we still have hobbies, work, and fortes; they might be in unexpected areas.

I've chosen to challenge myself in many ways and have enjoyed learning new skills. When I've faced challenges I haven't chosen, it's been important for me to find perspective.

Takeaways

- Keep learning.
- Try new things.
- If at first you don't succeed, trying again might be a good strategy. Recognizing there's an incompatibility that won't be overcome and then pivoting to something else might also be in order. There's no shame in that; celebrate your efforts and small successes you achieved, even if you couldn't attain your ultimate goal.

Thirteen
PERSPECTIVE

Keeping everything in perspective is essential when living with multiple comorbidities. I feel hopeful when I reflect on the blessings in my life despite and also because of difficulty. More hope comes when I am able to encourage others who may be going through a difficult time themselves. And I can live with an optimistic outlook when I remember to view my circumstances in a positive light, reminding myself that Someone has been working in the background all along, bringing joy and good even in the midst of trials.

Because of Versus in Spite Of

Sometimes people express to me how impressed they are with what I can do *in spite of* or *despite* having MS. (I'm picking MS because it seems to be what everyone assumes is the biggest obstacle I face.) It's true that I have MS and other challenges and face barriers as a result. Perhaps it's remarkable that I've done what I have within this context. However, some wonderful things have happened to me that wouldn't have happened had I not had MS. These are blessings that have occurred *because of* not *in spite of* my neurological condition. There have been two significant "because of" graces in my life.

SAHM

Having the opportunity to stay at home with Claire was a significant blessing and one that would likely not have happened without my MS diagnosis. We've never lived in poverty or indulged in a lavish lifestyle. Our middle-class household would have had a harder time making ends meet on only one salary. Because I deal with profound fatigue, I became eligible for long-term disability benefits. My benefit amount wasn't as much as my salary would have been had I continued teaching full-time, but it made a big difference, especially considering we now had some increased medical costs. I live in Canada, and we do have free health care that pays for most of our medical expenses. However, even though much of the cost of my disease-modifying therapy was covered, the amount we were responsible for was still significant to us.

I wasn't jumping for joy at being diagnosed with MS because it gave me a free ride to be lazy and not do anything with myself. MS happened. I couldn't change that. One of the consequences of having this disease was receiving long-term disability benefits, and this contributed to my being able to be a stay-at-home mom to Claire. I received benefits because I needed to make accommodations for the disabling effect MS had on my energy. As noted in the chapter on fatigue, I napped every day. I also had long nights. I "slept when the baby slept" plus threw in a nap every afternoon. And when debilitating relapses occurred, I often needed to call in reinforcements to help me cope. Staying at home was not a case of simply subtracting work and playing with dolls all day with my little girl. The actual formula was more as follows: subtract work, add care for a small human, manage a household with fewer energy resources than before having MS, add manage new symptoms and appointments, and constantly deal with guilt that I wasn't present enough for my husband and daughter. I continue to appreciate all the help I have received.

Always the Teacher
Even when I haven't been a classroom teacher, I seem to have sought out opportunities to teach others whenever possible. My poor little sister had to contend with worksheets I made for her to occupy her on a road trip, and when I should easily have known better, in my forties I thought it would be a fantastic idea to start a grammar blog. It turns out that people don't seek out grammar lessons for free or for hire, and young sisters usually just want to enjoy a road trip on their summer vacation without homework assignments imposed on them.

Being a piano teacher has been a much more productive way for me to give instruction. I have poured myself into my teaching and invested love and energy into the students in my studio. I've enjoyed developing new ways of looking at the challenges of note-naming and making simple compositions. Teaching students one-on-one is a great privilege. I love being part of the lives of young children, adolescents, and adults from twenty to sixty years old. It's wonderful to be able to cater to the specific needs of each aspiring musician who sits on my piano bench. Teaching a few of Claire's friends along the way has been a joy and a lovely way to enter her world. I've had meaningful heart-to-heart conversations with some of the teen girls I've taught, and I cherish the time I spend each week with two of my nieces, with whom I hadn't made a significant connection before piano lessons.

THIRTEEN: PERSPECTIVE

When I worked in the classroom, I was a homeroom teacher with a focus on the core subjects of English, math, science, and social studies. The resource teachers were usually the ones who worked with students with additional needs at a micro level. In my studio, I fill this role and have loved the challenge of finding new ways to break down concepts and instill confidence in children who often face barriers and discouragements at school. Two of these children have also dealt with health challenges and have had corresponding difficulties in learning in the same way and at the same pace as their classmates. Parents, students, and teacher are all grateful for the opportunity afforded us in setting the pace individually in an environment that has time to celebrate the achievements of each individual without attention drawn to the progress of other students.

My students feel like an extension of my family, and as we have lessons in our home, Kevin and Claire have gotten to know each one to varying extents. I sense the precious young souls who sit on my piano bench have a sense of family with me too, as I receive enthusiastic hugs from almost every student each week. One of these members of my music family is dear David. I had a long phone conversation with his mom, Shannon, before we began lessons. She spoke candidly about how David can be more reserved due to his personality and also because of the impact being on the autism spectrum has had on how he relates to others. He was quiet at our first lessons, and Shannon sat in a chair on the other side of the piano bench until he felt comfortable at lessons without her present.

Seemingly unrelated to piano, between the first and second years of teaching David, I learned to solve the Rubik's cube. A month after acquiring this skill, I showed him how to solve one; soon he was solving it faster than I was. It has been enjoyable to share both piano and cubing with him. A pleasant consequence of him learning to cube is that David went on to make friends at school with other boys with a similar interest. Who knew that piano lessons would lead to cubing, which would lead to a boost to David's social life? This is another example of something that might seem like a coincidence but actually feels exactly like something God would orchestrate.

More than cubing or coding or Roblox, David loves piano. It has become what he wants to do when he grows up. He lights up whenever I play any piece I've been working on, and he says that hearing me play is one of the best parts of the lesson. He knows how to butter me up! Actually, his sparkling blue eyes are all it takes for me to feel special around him.

One year when he was still in the beginner books, he had learned and memorized over ten pieces. I hosted a "David-cital" for him in front of his family and a handful of others who are close to him. They were a small but enthusiastic audience. The event was one in which David felt safe to leave his comfort zone and be the performer. It likely helped that all the people present had eavesdropped when he was playing at home or at their houses.

The highlight of the whole June 2023 recital for me was when Shannon told David to stand with me for a picture at the conclusion of the event. The words she used to address him went something like, "David. Go stand next to your best girl." Sometimes just before David comes over, Claire will ask, "What time is your best friend coming over?"

David's mom has also become a friend of mine. We share some similar challenges with migraines and low energy stores. When I think back over the last twenty or so years, it feels unimaginable to me that all this was not orchestrated by God. He allowed me to get MS, which changed my life in profound ways, not the least of which being the opportunity to stay home with Claire and have positive interactions with children, teens, and parents. Shannon thinks their family is on the receiving end of all the benefits of the student-teacher relationship. My family can corroborate my statement that having David in my life on a weekly basis is a legitimate benefit to me too. Being someone's best girl is rather amazing, and my life is richer and more joy-filled with David in it.

Conversations

I've appreciated being able to have unique conversations with others in similar situations. When people know that you legitimately understand what they're going through because you've been there, or maybe are still there yourself, they tend to open up fairly easily. I've found myself engaged in deep conversations with others—conversations we haven't necessarily had with those close to us in family or friendship. It's an honour when people open up to me, because I know it takes courage to speak vulnerably about personal trials. This reminds me of two Bible verses in the New Testament:

> Praise be to the God and Father of our Lord Jesus Christ, the Father of compassion and the God of all comfort, [4]who comforts us in all our troubles, so that we can comfort those in any trouble with the comfort we ourselves receive from God. (2 Corinthians 1:3–4)

I love these verses. They speak about God's compassion and comfort, both of which I have experienced personally. He has absolutely been a comfort to me in my *"troubles,"* and I can praise him as I acknowledge this even while in the middle of unpleasant circumstances. It humbles me to know I have been able to offer comfort to others.

I'm Medicated Too

As I mentioned in the "It's All Right to Cry" chapter, our society's awareness of mental illness has increased in recent years. I don't love having clinical depression, but I am grateful it's been used as a way to connect with others in a similar boat. I'm often amazed how easily people share their struggles with mental health when I open the door by mentioning something about mine. Sometimes I'll be talking to someone I haven't really spoken to much before, and I sense they may be experiencing depression or anxiety. I can often find an easy and natural way to work into the conversation that I take antidepressants or have struggled with anxiety. Often the other person completely relaxes and opens up about their current circumstances and mental health. I'm also willing to share about my experiences with counselling and how talk therapy has been useful to me in dealing with anxious or unhealthy thoughts.

You might be thinking that disclosing antidepressant-use or being in therapy don't seem like easy or natural topics to weave into a casual discussion. I'm not embarrassed about this part of my medical history and find it both easy and natural to talk about in the right context. I don't stand on a street corner and announce my chemical imbalances to everyone in earshot. And I will not steer happy and lighthearted conversations into dark and dreary places just for the opportunity to mention my own depression or anxiety experiences. If I'm wrong about my feelings that my conversation partner is dealing with mental illness, there are no losers as far as I'm concerned. The other person may feel awkward at first, hearing me open up about something personal that has been a taboo subject in the past. But I am determined that mental illness should be something spoken of as easily as physical illness.

Assistive Device Solidarity

I like to make positive comments about people's assistive devices when I encounter them. Expressing solidarity can relax people and offer validation that they're not alone. I've gone up to people, mostly ones in their senior years, as they seem to comprise the biggest demographic of assistive device-users, and made comments such as:

- I like that big storage basket on your walker. My walker doesn't have that. I love my walker, but it doesn't have as many extras because I had to prioritize getting one as light as possible.

- <holding the door open for someone using a mobility scooter> I understand how awkward it can be to get through doorways in a scooter. Mine is quite large, and I fear I am not always the best driver! I admire how you reversed so easily.
- Can I ask you a question? It seems using a cane might benefit me in walking more easily. What do you like about yours? I'd need mine to help with balance as well as support when I become fatigued and weak. Does yours help in any of those ways?
- <After approaching a young woman sitting next to a walker in the airport.> "Is that your walker?" <After she confirmed that it was, I went on to say,> "When I got my walker, I posted a picture of it and came across other young people with the same walker who used the hashtag #BabesWithMobilityAids." She loved hearing about that and was determined to check out the hashtag on social media. She noticed my AFO and even knew exactly what to call it because she had two of her own. We shared our stories about how we "ended up" in the situations we're in today. It seems we've both learned the value of resilience and maintaining a positive attitude. It was obvious we enjoyed talking to someone who could approach these matters without dripping with sympathy for the other. We both know that's not productive, and it was a much better use of our time to learn more about each other's stories and just to smile and laugh together.

I have never had anyone respond to these comments negatively or awkwardly. They usually light up and are happy to talk about their assistive device with me. I think people of more advanced years feel tickled to be approached in this way by someone they perceive as young.

Normalizing

Normalizing is one of my favourite words. Once, I had a home visit from an occupational therapist who helped me set up the workstations I use around my home. I needed ergonomic solutions, and she had great insights.

Fun fact: Did you know that the French word for occupational therapy is *ergothérapie*? Even if you're unfamiliar with French, you'll be able to spot the prefix "ergo" followed by what looks like a misspelling of therapy. Occupational therapy is all about ergonomics and helping clients function better at home and work. The only reason I know the word *ergothérapie* is because my French-speaking daughter wants to pursue a career in this field.

As we were analyzing my computer work station, I said something about me not being *normal*. She quickly jumped in to say, "Uh-uh. We don't use that word." Her kind scolding was a good reminder for me to stop comparing myself to others.

It seems *normal* is an unfitting word, so why is *normalizing* acceptable? For me, I experience *normalizing* when people act in a way that sees me as a person first, without a focus on disability. And when the world is easier for me to navigate because thoughtful accessibility measures have been considered and implemented, I feel my disability causes me to stand out a lot less. I am empowered to engage in activities and gatherings more easily without drawing attention to the way I walk. An example of this is feeling as though I stuck out like a sore thumb because I couldn't get my scooter or rollator through a heavy door easily. Others notice what appears to be turning into a major fiasco just to enter a building. I've been treated well and have received help from others to navigate a door obstacle. But when I can press a magic button that will open a door and allow me to walk or roll into a building with ease, I experience a feeling of being treated as an equal. I can enter as Robyn and not as *Disabled Woman*.

Letting Go

Warning: sensitive material about a tragedy involving a child follows.

On November 30, 1984, something happened that rocked my hometown of Winnipeg. A thirteen-year-old girl disappeared on her way home from school; the city was soon plastered with signs that said, "Have You Seen Candace?" The following January, the search for Candace came to a close with the discovery of her frozen body. Candace's parents, Cliff and Wilma Derksen, and her siblings, Odia and Syras, were suddenly living in a different world than the one they woke up to on the morning of that fateful November day. It became clear that Candace had been murdered, and now Cliff and Wilma would begin receiving the chilling label of "parent of a murdered child." Candace's mom, Wilma, put pen to paper, and in the early 1990s, published her first book, *Have You Seen Candace?* In it, she takes her reader through her perspective surrounding the events of the day that Candace was abducted to the anniversary of these events one year later. I have read *Have You Seen Candace?* and was moved by her candid retelling of what she went through.

Wilma went on to become involved in helping families who have gone through similar experiences. She has facilitated restorative justice sessions with offenders to foster communication between those who committed the crimes and the people who became victims as a result. I have a friend who was involved in this process with Wilma, and he spoke positively about his experience tackling restorative justice with her.

Some years later, Wilma came out with another book, which also impacted me. This book is called, *The Way of Letting Go*. Early on, she and her husband chose to forgive the man who took their daughter's life. *The Way of Letting Go* is a book about forgiveness, grief, and learning to let go in fifteen different areas, including a happy ending, guilt and blame, self-pity, fear, and expectations that life is fair.

My circumstances are different from Derksens'. I can't relate to losing a child. Thinking about what the Derksen family has gone through quickly puts my health troubles into perspective. I appreciated the way she walked the reader through her process of letting go and how she acknowledged and didn't dismiss the difficulties she's faced. I am learning to do this—to acknowledge what I am experiencing and to let go of certain dreams and expectations.

I still struggle in many areas, but I will speak to my progress, giving examples related to each of the health challenges I have addressed so far.

Chronic migraine. I've come to more of a resigned acceptance than a letting go with respect to my headaches. At times I hesitate to go to an event due to *brain pain*. Some of the time, there really is no option but to stay at home in a quiet, dark room. Those are the headaches with acute phono- or photosensitivity. Other times I might reason: *I can be in pain at home or at church. The pain won't change, but I know I can put on a brave face and grin and bear it for a short time.* Some people have expressed to me that they can't believe what I do while in pain. But we don't know how we'll cope with something until we're put in that position. They would likely rise to the occasion more gracefully than they imagine. Also, I could turn around and tell them that they don't see what goes on behind the scenes. Others don't see how much time I've had to spend in bed to get to the place where I could be "up and at 'em." Some days a shower won't happen, or at least not for many hours after I had hoped. I might spend an hour before teaching a piano lesson with my Cefaly vibrating my trigeminal nerve. And after the lesson, quite possibly I will be back in bed.

MS. Most of the time, I'm content with and accept the fact that I will no longer enjoy a long walk with a friend as I have in the past. Kevin has wanted to go on a holiday to New York City for years. That's a walking holiday if I've ever heard of one. It feels heavy to me to think that I'm the reason we won't be able to do that together. However, when I expressed this to him, his response was reassuring and supportive. Those two adjectives don't do justice to how he makes me feel. Basically,

MS is the reason, not Robyn. Kevin told me that when something happens to me, it is happening to us. I can't imagine being married to anyone who's more of a team player than that! He reminds me that I didn't choose to be ill, and feeling guilty about the impact it has on others isn't necessary or expected.

> *Kevin told me that when something happens to me, it is happening to us.*

Clinical depression. Remarkably, this has been the easiest one to accept, because although it doesn't have a cure, it has proven to be the most treatable of my main ailments. I've often said, "I'm clinically depressed but happily medicated. Most of the time." I am happy and grateful there are medications and therapy to help those who experience mental illness, myself included. Although antidepressants don't automatically switch on my happy face, they make a difference in how I experience life, with the result being many more smiles than would occur without their use. During my darkest days, days I wasn't on medication for depression, I wouldn't have felt the same way. The darkness took a front seat to everything else going on.

IBS. I really don't enjoy limiting what I eat, but choosing to not eat foods containing gluten or onions isn't hard when I consider the negative consequences of not sticking to the low FODMAP diet. Whereas my headaches frustrate and discourage me, IBS annoys me, sometimes to the point of being frustrated and discouraged. I think I have "risen above" self-pity in other areas but am still having trouble totally accepting the challenges I face with IBS. I long to be "normal" and be able to eat anything. Remembering that IBS symptoms are worse than the Low FODMAP diet helps keep the condition in perspective, and I have mostly let go of being able to eat certain foods. When Krispy Kreme Doughnuts came to my city, how much I have mentally let go of eating gluten may have been in question.

There are also reminders of realities in our lives that remain permanently changed because of my physical limitations. It can be triggering to see people sharing posts on social media of their family with multiple children going on a long hike together on a summer day. This isn't something I'm able to do anymore, and seeing other people experiencing these moments reminds me of what's been taken. I'm happy for my friends and family who are able to have these adventures, but it's hard not to notice that I am not having similar outings with my family.

The silliest example of something I found triggering was watching Meg Ryan float quickly down the steps in the movie *You've Got Mail*. In fact, when I see people on TV or in reality walk up and down stairs easily without using anything for support, I *always* notice. I am forever changed and constantly need to work on letting go of wishing I easily did what others do so naturally. I certainly wouldn't want everyone to be in my shoes. I'm grateful Kevin is adept at navigating stairs for his sake and because in the absence of a handrail or bannister, he's my ticket to get up and down safely. I can let go of family-hike- or staircase-ease-envy when I remember the endless list of blessings I experience.

Comparisons

Comparisons get people into trouble. It's often tempting to compare myself or my circumstances to what I believe are normal ones. Normal can be a dangerous word when someone looks at the circumstances of others and decides that they don't measure up. I've had to learn not to compare myself to other mothers, wives, women my age, people with my education, and the list could go on. It's important to put these matters into perspective and remember the assurance I have that Kevin and Claire love me and the wife and mother I am to them. They often remind me of my many valuable contributions to our family and all I do that others do not or cannot.

One comparison that has been an especially ridiculous one that I've allowed myself to explore is comparing myself to other MS patients. I've heard of people with MS who have completed triathlons or even just go on regular runs. I find this astonishing! Those activities don't represent realistic options for me. In my case, it would be a TRYathlon, and the only event I might complete would be a slow and exhausting walk around the block. I need the perspective to remember that MS affects each patient differently. We have different strengths and weaknesses; we will no doubt experience our worlds and diseases in different ways.

Once, I had an encounter that surprised me because it revealed to me that others use me to gain perspective on their own circumstances. Some might assume they're doing better than I am because they're not facing what I'm dealing with. There's an assumption that they could never be happy or function as they would like to if they were dealing with what I encounter. And usually they're just comparing themselves to the MS part of this whole story. When I'm asked how I'm doing and reply that I am happy, I think they can't imagine themselves being happy in my shoes.

If

"If" is a small word, but it can have a big impact for better or worse, depending on one's perspective. I was listening to a sermon from December 12, 2021, given by Pastor Cam Stephens of Grant Memorial Church in Winnipeg, Canada. He was preaching on the story of the man who was paralyzed and lowered through the roof of a house by four friends in order to gain an audience with Jesus. These individuals acted in faith, and their trust in Jesus was made evident by the extreme measure they took by digging through a roof to get to Jesus. Jesus knew exactly why this patient had been presented to him. Many who approached him sought physical healing. However, in his omniscience, he also knew that what this man needed was more significant than physical healing; he knew he needed spiritual healing, namely forgiveness and to be made right with God. I believe this is ultimately the greatest need of all of us.

Pastor Cam encouraged his listeners to evaluate the way we view our own circumstances. Are we caught up thinking life will only work out if certain events happen? If only I met the right person. If only I were free of cancer. If only … We all have ways we might finish that statement. Instead of thinking "if only," what would it look like to consider our circumstances in terms of "even if"? Everything will be okay, even if my relationship status doesn't change or my cancer never goes into remission. I was grateful to Pastor Cam for a new way to look at an aspect of perspective I've spent many years thinking about.

Value

It's been said that we're our own worst critics. This definitely becomes apparent in the music world. After a recital or concert, performers may make reference to all the mistakes they made. Meanwhile, the audience members thoroughly enjoyed the performance and didn't notice anything was amiss. I know I've been apologetic of my performances after recitals and certainly have given accolades to many people who insisted their solo was second-rate. Graciously accepting compliments is something easier said than done, but it's always the classier road to take over itemizing everything that went wrong.

I need to apply this to life in general, and specifically when it comes to where I find my value. I find it difficult to graciously accept that I have worth when what I see so often are my shortcomings, or at least my perception of them. This relates to what I shared about making unhealthy comparisons. It's important to remind ourselves that we have worth. Hopefully you're surrounded by people on your team who remind you of this often. I think I'm often valued by my people more than I value myself. I can too easily assume that my life, that *I*, would have more worth if I could "do all the things"—cook all the suppers, do all the housework, etc. I can always use a perspective check when it comes to how I measure my worth, my value, and what makes me acceptable.

Putting My Best Foot Forward

A number of years ago, I got on the fitness tracker bandwagon and bought my first watch that tracked various aspects of my activity, including how many steps I took. It was amusing to see how many steps my feet logged in a day and a fun challenge to see if I could walk even more the next day. Walking ten thousand steps seems to have become the official mark of a successfully active day, and I have achieved that at least a handful of times. You can be sure two ten-thousand-step days in a row (or even in the same week or month) were not accomplished, though. Without a doubt, I would have needed significant recovery time after one of those epic activity days.

In this context, comparisons can be motivating and entertaining, especially when comparing to one's own past activity. As already noted, the times I have compared myself to others have often led to discouragement. When I look back, comparing my step count to my former progress hasn't always been productive either. MS is a progressive illness, and it's not surprising my walking ability and endurance would slowly decline over time. At the time of writing this, my daily step goal is around 1,500 steps. There are days when I reach over 3,000, but they aren't frequent and are always followed by a more sedentary day or two. If my step total is in the 2,000 to 2,500 range, my body will notice the extra push and beg for an early bedtime. I'm doing my best to be realistic while still pushing myself to keep moving, even when it's difficult to feel motivated. And I make a conscious effort not to say internally or out loud that my modest amount of walking is pathetic.

I've come up with a great hack for not getting discouraged about my daily step count. I've set my daily goal at just 250 steps. On a migraine day that sees me in bed more than I'd like—whether due to using the Cefaly or just to get rest—250 steps might even be a push. However, on a more average day for me, I like to "collect" 250-step units and try to get to six of those units. When we were on a holiday early in 2024, I managed to squeak out fifteen units in one day. This was one of those times I knew I'd pay for it in the following days, especially because the previous day had also been taxing. However, the experiences I had while achieving all those units made the fallout worth it.

Regular exercise is known to be important in maintaining mobility and in slowing decline. This was reinforced to me at my first appointment with Dr. Saab. Hearing this again was actually even more motivating than my watch vibrating while it cheers for me because I reached my step goal.

THIRTEEN: PERSPECTIVE

There are definitely benefits and pitfalls to having a daily reminder of my activity level. One of the best perks was apparent when I relayed to my neurologist how active I'd been. I told him that years ago, I managed 10,000 steps in one day on occasion; a few years ago, my number would have been comfortable around the 3,000 mark, and now my realistic goal is 1,500. That gave him a clear picture of my abilities and stamina over time. We discussed activity level and maintaining mobility and concluded that 1,500-step days regularly will pay dividends. I'm learning not to place my value on the "points" my watch tells me I've earned. Looking back at a week, noting trends helps me to understand how I was feeling and coping. A low-step day could mean a day I was in bed for much of the time with a migraine or recovering from a cold. A high-step day, especially if followed by a much lower one, tells me I was likely pushing myself too hard and was probably too busy. I'm learning to use this as a tool for motivation and also insight. And I'm always learning how to view and love myself better and press on with keeping myself moving.

You could say that my fitness tracker can be used as an instrument to give me perspective and helpful feedback *if* the results shown are always digested with a balanced view of my circumstances on a given day or week. Some people know they've been active in their day by their sore feet or aching muscles. Apparently, I appreciate a digital display to reflect similar information. One day, perhaps I'll grow up, but for now I enjoy being rewarded with these "stickers" for my efforts.

I've shared about some needed perspective as it relates to my four main health complaints. To keep my life extra interesting, I actually have quite a number of comorbidities not yet discussed. Usually, these have little direct impact on my day-to-day life except that they add to the pile of things I need to manage.

Takeaways

- Cherish time with your children.
- Be fully engaged in your work and don't minimize what you do. I am not *just* a piano teacher; I'm a piano teacher!
- If you've gone through something difficult or are living with a chronic condition, reflect on what has helped you. If you're with someone at an earlier stage of a similar journey, can you offer meaningful care to them?
- Be real. When you take risks to be vulnerable and honest, others are more likely to share about their reality. You might be able to help and encourage each other.
- Show sincere solidarity.
- Embrace normalizing, but avoid comparing yourself or others to a perceived "normal" standard.
- Take time to grieve losses of opportunities relating to a change in your reality. Eventually, work toward letting go of ideals you've had. The world isn't idyllic, and we need to learn to live positively in the circumstances in which we find ourselves.
- Don't minimize the need for grief.
- Throw comparisons out the window! No two people and no two situations are the same.
- Name your emotions accurately, and don't exaggerate.
- Replace "if only" thinking with "even if."
- If you are a person, you have value. You may need to redefine what you think valuable characteristics in a person are. God made you. On purpose. You are of infinite value to God and always will be.
- Use tools and technology wisely. Are they motivating you or causing you discouragement?

Fourteen
MORE-BIDITIES

I have multiple comorbidities, which is a morbid medical term to describe two or more medical conditions in the same patient. It can be overwhelming to manage, but I feel hopeful when I recognize all the care I've received. I am faced with many inconveniences, and I am grateful that I have been able to navigate managing them. There have been more solutions than problems, and that continues to give me hope.

Hypothyroidism
In November 2011, I was diagnosed with an underactive thyroid, or hypothyroidism. I think the main symptom I presented with was increased fatigue. My version of hypothyroidism is as convenient as a health problem can get. As long as I take a small pill once per day, my thyroid function isn't a concern. Besides daily medication, all that's required of me is to get my thyroid function checked annually, which is simply a test included in the blood work I get done for my yearly physical. I take the pill with other pills I take at the same time of day, so all my obligations to my thyroid are packaged with activities I'd do otherwise. I haven't noted any side effects with the prescription. For me, this has been an easy condition to deal with.

Others may find hypothyroidism to be much more problematic, though. I have three friends whose thyroid glands have been completely removed. As a result, they rely on medication to do all the regulating in their bodies that a thyroid gland is supposed to. If they were to miss a dose, it would have a much greater impact on them than it would on me if I accidentally skip my thyroid medication once in a while.

Hypotension
Another small health problem is that I tend to have low blood pressure (known as *hypotension* in the medical world). The disease-modifying therapy I'm on, Gilenya, can actually raise blood pressure, so continuing to run a low blood

pressure even while taking Gilenya is an indication of my body's stubbornness to keep a low profile. Two different doctors have advised me to "medicate" with salt. So with all the misplaced guilt I have about ridiculous matters, I actually feel no guilt about salting my mashed potatoes. When my blood pressure dips, I am definitely more fatigued, find myself sleeping more, and feel as if everything is more of an effort as I drag myself through the day. Again, this is fairly easy to manage; I season my food with salt and avoid getting up too fast from sitting or lying positions. My kidney function tests report healthy kidneys; if sodium were to affect an aspect of my health negatively, I would re-evaluate how I season my food.

Reflux

It's good that I'm not looking for anyone's sympathy because this next condition is also not exactly a major concern. The symptoms leading up to being diagnosed felt quite concerning, though, because they included chest pain. I saw a cardiologist and underwent a stress test. My heart was in great shape, and after starting to take medication daily for reflux, my symptoms disappeared. This pharmaceutical treatment has also not come with any negative side effects and is conveniently taken at the same time as other medications.

Desert Conditions

I have both dry eyes and dry mouth. These are relatively easy to manage as well. I take prescription eye drops twice per day. In three years, I think I've missed two doses, so I'm apparently managing the intervention.

The most effective treatment for dry mouth is a product containing xylitol, which is an IBS trigger. As a result, I sip water as needed. Dry mouth can contribute to dental problems, but apparently the two to three times per day I brush my teeth and my nightly flossing have been sufficient in keeping cavities away.

Chronic Insomnia

When I entered middle age, I began to have a lot of trouble falling asleep and staying asleep. It was definitely affecting my energy and productivity. I was prescribed another medication, which I took before bed every day. I was resistant to this intervention because I certainly didn't want to be addicted to sleeping pills! Soon after this treatment was initiated, I spoke to a family doctor I know and asked him if I should be concerned. He assured me the approach my doctor was taking was appropriate, and I wasn't abusing sleeping pills, as I had an actual sleep disorder. This gave me more peace of mind. Since being given the prescription, I methodically lowered my dose over time and weaned from it completely in 2024. Another option I was given was to try cannabis. I ruled it out quickly due to possible interactions and contraindications, expense, and not wanting my dreams to become more vivid than they already are.

Fake Sports Injury

The activities I gravitate to and ones that play to my strengths aren't exactly in the high-performance sports category. In order to obtain a sports injury, I dedicated myself to many hours of piano practice and drilled twenty-four scales in a variety of forms at a quick tempo. The result was bilateral epicondylitis, also known as tennis elbow, in both arms. This is aggravated by activities such as typing, knitting, and crocheting, which I have spent many hours doing. I no longer engage in needlework, but writing this book has seen me at the keyboard more than usual. Extended time spent typing or playing piano will make the tennis elbow flare up, and a bizarre consequence of this condition is that when I hold a cold object with my hand, I have pain in my elbow. Shaving cold carrots is uncomfortable, and I do well to plan ahead and take them out of the fridge in advance and not just immediately before needing to prepare them. The intense piano playing I did to cause all of this occurred in my teens and early twenties. I am still feeling the effects two and a half decades later. I've been to both physical and athletic therapy for this injury.

De Quervain's Tenosynovitis

In my forties, I added to my arm injury situation by acquiring De Quervain's tenosynovitis. The epicondylitis caused forearm and elbow pain, and the pain from this one is more in my thumb and wrist, mainly only in my left arm. Curiously, this was possibly caused by the foot drop in my right leg. I'm right-handed, but I have subconsciously shifted carrying tasks to my left hand and arm, as my right leg is weak and doesn't love it when I overload my right side. This shift has put more pressure on my left upper limb. I've seen a physiotherapist for this and wore a specialized brace when the pain was at its peak. It seems to have resolved for the most part but is also willing to be symptomatic on occasion. Stretching, rest, and the brace are all helpful. Honestly, one of my biggest challenges with De Quervain's tenosynovitis is remembering how to pronounce it.

Kidney Stone

Kidney stones are nothing to laugh about as they have a reputation for causing pain on par with childbirth. This is why in 2010, when a urologist reported the results of a recent bladder and kidney ultrasound and casually mentioned I had a kidney stone in my right kidney, my response was, "Excuse me. Say what now?

Let's just circle back to that before we move on." Apparently it isn't uncommon for people to have kidney stones and be oblivious about their existence. They were an incidental finding on an ultrasound prescribed to investigate other concerns. No measures have ever been taken to rid me of my little rocky renal friend, but I've been monitored with more ultrasound and CT scans. I had imaging done at some point before the last CT scan, which showed that the stone had increased in size, such that it wouldn't likely pass easily if it finally decided to journey into the nearby ureter. This was all unsettling. Given that I had a kidney stone and once had a high calcium oxalate crystal count in a urinalysis, I was advised to eat a low-oxalate diet. This was unbelievably exciting news for me to hear. Please note sarcasm.

There were already numerous limits to my diet, and now I needed to manage the mysterious oxalate content in my food. I started to research and take note of how my food scored in the oxalate department and was finding it tedious. I even hired my favourite dietician to help me navigate this new reality. Thankfully, not too long after this revelation, I saw a new urologist and told him how I was approaching my food choices. He gave me permission to relax completely about oxalates as long as I avoided spinach and rhubarb. Those two vegetables seemed so random, but they are the big winners when it comes to oxalate content, with scores more than ten times that of most others. I was sad to have to omit spinach, because as someone who has trouble enjoying vegetables, spinach was one I could enjoy in a salad, in spinach-artichoke dip, cooked in lasagna, or in an egg breakfast. Lettuce is usually an easy substitute, though, so it hasn't been a massive loss. But as a Mennonite who loves a rhubarb pie, a dessert called rhubarb platz (like a coffee cake with fruit and crumbs), and the meringue dessert famous in Mennonite circles and often simply called *rhubarb dessert*, this was harder news to swallow (pardon the pun).

Get ready for some exciting news. My last CT scan showed no evidence of kidney stones. I challenged the doctor who went over the results with me because it seemed completely implausible. I was convinced that I would notice passing a kidney stone as large as mine apparently was. So this one is sort of a fake health problem because it seems to have completely disappeared. Do I continue avoiding spinach and rhubarb because of my sordid history with my kidney stone?

TMD

I've had trouble with my **temporomandibular joints** (TMJ) for years. When someone has a dysfunction with these joints, they earn the badge of having a temporomandibular disorder (TMD). When I was nineteen, pain in the joints in my jaw increased to the point where I could only open my mouth about three centimetres, or just over one inch. This made eating difficult and found me wedging and squishing food past my teeth in order to consume anything. I saw my dentist for this, and he had a splint (also called an appliance or night guard) made for me. I was required to wear the splint whenever I wasn't eating or brushing my teeth. My symptoms didn't resolve as was hoped, and I eventually had surgery on one side of the joint to clean up scar tissue that had formed.

After time, TMJ physiotherapy, and continued wearing of the splint, I was able to resume mostly normal biting and chewing behaviours. I was advised to go on a soft diet and avoid such pleasures as biting into an apple and chewing gum. Since that time, my jaw has continued to make delightful clicking and popping noises when I have pushed it to its wee limits. Tough food such as steak can still be a challenge, and when issues resurface, I'm able to keep matters under control with exercises and stretches.

Why did this happen to me? Bruxism happened. Bruxism is a term dentists use to describe naughty behaviours like jaw-clenching and teeth-grinding. I do both and sleep with a significant night guard. I clenched so hard I broke my previous appliance. After that, my dentist had another one made for me that was shockingly thick. When he handed it to me, he said, "Robyn, this is not a challenge." Tension or stress is the reason often given for why people engage in bruxism.

The Great Recession
This next one might be worth skipping if you're squeamish about pain and blood, but before you jump ahead to "Management Degree," I'll give a quick non-gory summary. I will let you know when the dramatic part is about to begin.

Continuing on the dental theme, I'll shift focus from my jaw to my gingiva. My gums have slowly receded, possibly due to multiple factors. Bruxism, orthodontic braces, and aggressive brushing may have all contributed. Gum recession was first noted by a dentist in the early 2000s. At that time, he explained that if the recession became much worse, a gum graft could be performed whereby tissue would be taken from my palate and grafted into the gum line where recession had occurred. I don't know which of the above three factors contributed most to my need to see a periodontist, but the past can't be changed. Going forward, I have altered my oral hygiene routine. I now use an electric toothbrush, which lets me know if I'm using too much pressure by making a different vibrating sound. It was a simple change to make, and I'm happy I adopted this new strategy to keep me in check.

I had one large graft over eight adjacent teeth. The surgery was a success, and I'm glad it has been done. However, there were some complications, and I had a much more difficult recovery than is typical. This is likely, in part, due to dealing with comorbidities. Apparently, my experience puts me in the 1 per cent range of what gum graft patients go through. I feel so special and elite. If you find yourself in the squeamish category, this might be a good time to jump ahead to the "Management Degree" section.

The actual gum graft procedure wasn't traumatic. Pain was manageable, but after a week, I started having palatal bleeds, which I was able to control by applying pressure through a wet tea bag (the tannins and caffeine stimulate clotting) and layers of gauze. However, a few days later I ended up with an uncontrolled arterial bleed in my palate. I ended up staying overnight in the Urgent Care department of a nearby hospital and was eventually treated the next morning in another hospital with an oral surgery department. The first time I ever assigned a pain level of ten was thanks to the oral surgery resident freezing my bleeding palate. My experience in labour and delivery didn't elicit a response even close to rivalling this. One of my favourite memes, which I saw for the first time a few months before, makes me laugh and reflects my feelings about freezing administered in a raw and damaged, bleeding palate:

Nurse:	How would you rate your pain?
Me:	Zero stars.
Nurse:	
Me:	Would not recommend.

An arterial bleed ten days after surgery, excessive bruising that extended from my lower lip and down my chest, and my profound swelling are all factors that contributed to my elite 1 per cent status. Swelling was expected, but mine was more significant than typical; one reason it may have become as considerable as it did was my inability to apply ice following the graft. Thanks to the effect of the oral sedation, I wasn't able to stay awake to follow through with the recommended icing routine that would have decreased the swelling. I do bruise easily, and because I had grafts below so many teeth, more bruising occurred. My appearance certainly caused concern among family and friends because it was indeed shocking. The arterial bleed was simply a random and unfortunate event. My healing and recovery were long and difficult, and this was likely due, at least in part, to the comorbidities I already contend with. When my graft stitches were removed, the dental assistant shared that another patient with MS had more trouble than usual in her recovery as well.

After living through much difficulty, lessons were learned:

- I added to my list of "things I had no idea I'd be able to endure." I wouldn't have predicted I'd be able to go through twenty-three hours of active labour and then endure five hours of pushing. I especially wouldn't have thought this could all happen while having MS, which has involved debilitating fatigue. And I most definitely wouldn't have believed that my TMD-self would be able to clench my jaw for thirteen hours straight in order to apply constant pressure to my bleeding palate while staying up through the night only to experience my first number ten on the pain scale the next morning.
- It's possible to have a sense of humour and be empathetic toward others while going through a traumatic event. My inclination to find humour and bring levity didn't escape with all the blood pouring out of my mouth. Kevin and I shared moments we could laugh at immediately, with other situations revealing some hilarity in retrospect.

  It was easy to feel empathetic toward other patients I met in Urgent Care. Thanks to the IV I received, I made many trips to the bathroom. I found myself walking by a young man and his dad numerous times. Through my sign language, I was able to discover a skateboard injury had brought them to the hospital, and I expressed my compassion for the long evening they were having. I was also glad to be able to show some care to my caregivers. I encountered four different nurses and two doctors during my ordeal. They were all kind and compassionate toward me, and I had the opportunity to show a note to one of the nurses that said: *Thank you for caring for me. I am praying you all have a good shift.*

  Because I couldn't speak to show my appreciation for the care I received, I would often stroke the hand of a nurse tending to me. I also stroked the hand of the oral surgery resident; this was done after the gauze was out of my mouth. He'd frozen my palate, and I'd said, "I don't like you very much!" My non-verbal expression of forgiveness came quickly once the freezing took effect, and my mouth was again full of hands working away.
- I learned to appreciate being able to eat and drink with ease. After I was treated in the hospital, my palate became engorged, and I had difficulty drinking, eating, and swallowing pills. When I could perform these behaviours easily again, I had a new appreciation for much I had taken for

granted. Once, Claire's friend inquired about how I was doing, and Claire answered, "Much better! She's eating crunchy cereal now!" Eating soggy cereal was already progress after days of soup and smoothies, but when I could eat cereal without soaking it in milk first, I was overjoyed.

- I began to understand, to a small degree, what having PTSD must be like. I became hypersensitive to any sensation in my mouth that I associated with feelings I had before the palatal bleeds. I also became fearful and paranoid when it came to palatal freezing. My anxiety level augmented substantially as complications increased. I think MS was one factor in my difficult recovery, but the background of mental illness definitely made psychological healing challenging. At one point a nurse asked me to rate my pain, and I expressed how it was actually quite low at that moment but wrote a note saying that the emotional pain was a ten out of ten. I'm thankful I have experienced healing both physically and emotionally. I'm sure I will always feel hesitation and fear whenever freezing in my mouth is required in the future, but I've learned I can face even that.

Two days after my hospital ordeal, I was able to see my periodontist. She was unhappy with the state of my palate and feared infection. The periodontist explained that ideally she'd like to freeze my palate, un-suture, debride incisions, and re-suture, but she didn't insist on that course of action. She didn't put any pressure on me but let me make an informed decision. I agreed to her plan, and the subsequent freezing, although still painful, was actually the easiest to endure of the three instances. I appreciated her patience, kindness, and gentleness. Also, she kept calling me "sweetheart," and I truly felt the endearing term was indicative of her compassion toward me in light of the unfortunate circumstances.

Polypharmaceutical Case

I wouldn't be the least surprised to learn that many who have read this far in the book are feeling uncomfortable and would really like to give me some advice about my apparent drug habit. There may appear to be no end to the number of prescriptions I'm willing to take. At an MS follow-up appointment a number of years ago, Dr. Marriott told me he'd like to see me taking the fewest medications and at the lowest doses possible. I loved this mindset and always make prescription drug choices with that perspective. I think carefully about which prescriptions are included in the monthly blister packs my pharmacy assembles for me. I appreciate Western medicine and the science and research it represents. As such,

I am not averse to taking remedies in the form of medications but always do so with careful thought and a weighing of the risks and rewards.

Management Degree

I've never desired to go into business or to become a manager. However, all of my major and minor health issues add up to a lifestyle that is far from carefree. There's so much I need to stay on top of that I do find it easy to become overwhelmed and, unsurprisingly, have dealt with anxiety as a result. Although I don't have a business degree, I certainly feel like a busy manager of the business of my health.

Takeaways

- Strive to stay on top of health concerns.
- Seek out appropriate therapy and do your best to follow through on any homework prescribed.
- Follow your doctor's instructions and take medications accordingly.
- Acknowledge when stresses are compounding and causing you to feel overwhelmed.
- Look for opportunities to smile and reach out to others, even when facing trials yourself. Something I have reminded myself often is *this too shall pass*.

Fifteen
TAKEAWAYS—À LA CARTE MENU

People are generally kind, well-meaning, and don't wish to offend others. My particular story includes mostly beautifully sensitive people whose actions and attitudes give me hope as they make sincere efforts to understand my circumstances. Below I will discuss how people could respond to various situations in helpful ways, as well as other interactions that would have room for growth.

Affirmations

What follows is a list of some of the comments people have made to me and my thoughts on whether they would be encouraging or feel insensitive.

- *"You looked like you were struggling."* I don't love hearing this. What I hear is I was being watched, and the speaker probably felt sorry for me. This is not helpful for me. If I am struggling and need help, simply ask if I'd like help, and I'll direct you as to how I'd like to receive your assistance. If I decline help, respect my wishes. And please stop staring at me through a lens of pity.
- *"Well, you look good."* I hear this frequently after talking to someone about my health. Often they've just discovered I have MS, and I get this compliment as a consolation prize. Would I look good if I looked the way I did and didn't have MS? If someone wants to give me a compliment, my preference is to receive it without a qualifier.
- *"I admire the way you deal with MS"*—right after we just had a long conversation about the impact my migraines have been having. Somehow all that my conversation partner heard was how hard MS is, even though I hadn't even mentioned neurological hardships. This is frustrating because it makes me feel as though I haven't really been listened to, and it minimizes the migraines, which Kevin has frequently said are more debilitating than MS. Sometimes I've had the whole, "Hi. How are you?" conversation with someone, and my reply has been completely positive. However, it seems in their mind they assumed I wasn't doing well and continued

the conversation on that premise—and usually I can tell they're thinking about my wellness in the context of MS. I try to be honest when I'm not doing well. If things aren't going fantastically, I'll often answer with one word: medium. Some people accept that, and others ask me what could be better. If I'm not doing well, it's usually due to *brain pain*, and I will relay my condition. This gives the other person the opportunity to be sensitive about noise and light and to understand why I might not be acting like my "normal" self.

- *"You're such an inspiration"* or *"You are such a strong person"* or *"I could never deal with what you're going through."* If you've thought that about others, you're certainly not alone. I know I have. You might be surprised at your resilience when you're put to the test one day. We are better at dealing with and getting through trials in the present than we think we will be in the hypothetical future.

> *We are better at dealing with and getting through trials in the present than we think we will be in the hypothetical future.*

This was certainly true for me while in labour and while dealing with painful complications from oral surgery. You might also be surprised to find out that people going through difficult circumstances don't tend to appreciate hearing that others admire their unimaginable strength and how inspiring they are. They're usually simply doing what needs to be done to get through an ordeal they haven't chosen.

Attitude
- Be positive and upbeat. Don't assume everything is bleak. There's a lot more to people than their health. Be curious about other parts of their life.
- Be hopeful and positive.
- If you're curious about someone's health, disability, or assistive devices, genuine curiosity is usually welcomed. I'm happy to answer questions and will go into as much detail as I think is appropriate for my audience. Negative curiosity should be avoided—the kind that makes someone feel like a spectacle or novelty. If you're that curious about something, search online, and you'll likely find a number of videos made by people who are choosing to show others, including strangers, how they handle situations related to their disability. And if you can't find any information or videos to satisfy your curiosity, that's probably a sign that the issue is a personal one and should remain that way.

Assumptions

There are a number of areas relating to my health where people have sometimes made inaccurate assumptions.

- Free time. Since I'm not working full-time, I must have oodles of free time, right? I'm actually a busy person, and sometimes what occupies me, out of necessity, is resting. I'm not the only one for whom assumptions might be made about free time. I've learned not to make assumptions about free time available to retired people, as well as those who are incarcerated.
- MS equals wheelchair. There's often a correlation between MS and inevitably needing a wheelchair. MS affects people differently, and while decreasing mobility might be common, it shouldn't be assumed. Not all MS patients use or will end up using this assistive device.
- I have also valued the insight I've gained through relationships with people affected by a couple of conditions outside of my experience and have outlined some of those thoughts below with their affirmation. The last matter is more personally relevant. The more I get to know others, the more I learn about circumstances beyond my small world, and the more I can relate with increased sensitivity to others. It's in that spirit that I share these thoughts on topics beyond my particular illnesses.

    —Autism is a disorder close to my heart. There can be a perception that autism equals savant equals non-verbal equals math genius. Thank you, *Rain Man*, for showing us one *rare* example of a life impacted by autism. You may have heard different terms for autism. Autism, autism spectrum disorder (ASD for short), Asperger's, neurodivergent, and "being on the spectrum" are all commonly used. I'm comfortable using any of these except Asperger's, as the term has been discontinued as a diagnosis. Neurodivergent is an umbrella term encompassing a number of conditions including autism and ADHD. All people with ASD are neurodivergent, but the reverse is not true.

    I know a number of people with autism, and they clearly show me there is definitely not one "autism mould." It truly is a spectrum disorder. The roster of my friends and acquaintances with autism include someone who would be considered non-verbal, a man who is married with children and was diagnosed as an adult, and many somewhere in between. My friend Shannon has two sons with autism; one is a young adult, and the other is my piano student, David, who is an adolescent. While there is some overlap, they experience ASD in different ways. I wouldn't classify either as a savant, but due to their high intelligence and excellent verbal skills, they're often labelled as "high-functioning." Labels put limits on people and are accompanied by unhelpful assumptions. The adult son is unlikely to be able to join the workforce but is denied funding because there's a perception that he can function to a superior degree. In reality, he struggles to leave the house and has few relationships outside his immediate family. His younger brother also has social challenges, but they manifest themselves differently.

—Weight. If my friend is morbidly obese, is it helpful to tell them to eat healthy and exercise? Likely the only things it would accomplish are an awkwardness in our friendship and their resentment of me. They will be all too aware of the solution you suggested, but the reasons they have become obese are likely complex and ones someone who has a healthy weight couldn't understand. Eating nutritiously and exercising may be a small part of what would be required to come to a healthy weight.

Speaking of weight, I want to address another faux pas. In Western culture, it's often assumed that thin is good, and fat is bad. There are places in the world where the opposite is the mindset. An overweight person can be a sign of wealth, as it implies the affording of ample food. At the other end of the spectrum, there are people who are underweight and don't wish to be. Steer clear of making comments such as, "Oh, you're so lucky to be thin. I'm so jealous." Being overweight or underweight is not always a choice a person has made. Either can be the result of medication side effects—often from life-saving medications. There have been times when I've lost 10 per cent of my body weight in a year as the result of many factors: altering my diet to accommodate intolerances, fatigue, and mood problems all being contributors.

Actions
- Don't deny that someone has a conspicuous disability or pretend you didn't notice. At the same time, don't stare at people you think are struggling, or draw attention to the "issue." Certainly if it's possible to help them (and they want help), be there to lend a hand. I have two stories to illustrate how

I appreciated the responses of others when I was in public and my mobility challenges were apparent:

—Kevin and I attended a funeral in a small church. When we arrived, Kevin dropped me off and then parked the car. It was a windy day, and after struggling a bit to open the heavy front door, I sort of blew into the building. I met a kind man at the top of the stairs who was acting as an usher.

After the service, I headed for the stairs leading to the basement, as I had noted that the restrooms were located downstairs. A woman came up to me and told me that there was a small bathroom on the main floor I'd be welcome to use. When I returned, she was standing with the usher I'd met before the service, and I went up to her to thank her for directing me to the facility that was much more accessible for me. It wasn't a typical accessibility restroom, as it was about the size of a closet, but it worked for my needs and provided me helpful access. It was clear that the kind woman who'd redirected me had seen me walking with what appeared to be a limp. I thanked her for not pretending my walking wasn't challenged. She commented on how unhelpful that would be, and I agreed. She did a few subtle but wonderful things: she didn't stare, she provided practical help without drawing attention to my condition, and she looked at me with friendliness and not condescension or pity. I found out she is married to the man I'd met earlier, and we had a lovely conversation in which I revealed MS was responsible for the wonky walking. They have a relative with MS, and it's clear they have a good understanding of how to relate to people with disabilities.

Kevin and I were on vacation in Florida and met up with my parents, who were at the end of a road trip. We spent the afternoon miniature golfing at an amazing pirate-themed course that was made to look like a mountain with caves. It was February and not hot by Florida standards, but as the day progressed, the temperature became too warm for me. I had dressed for the weather as perceived when I stepped onto a shaded balcony hours earlier. Wearing shorts instead of jeans would have made a difference to my heat tolerance. Coming from snowy Winnipeg apparently affected my ability to judge wardrobe needs in summer weather.

The amount of walking required to play one game of miniature golf wouldn't likely require a lot of exertion, but climbing "mountains" sure does. On about the fifteenth hole, I realized my body was done. I stopped playing the course and just focused on getting through walking to the end. The last climb was up a shallow staircase with deep treads. I began my ascent, trying to coax my leg with foot drop to pick itself up. Eventually, I got on my hands and knees and made my way crawling up the stairs. I was in survival mode and not worried about being a spectacle or drawing attention. At least, I wasn't until after the game when we were waiting for Daddy to pick us up with the car.

The women in the party that golfed after us had finished their game and were also talking just outside the eighteenth hole. I felt self-conscious that my antics had slowed down their game. I went over to the young women in this group and thanked them for their patience. I wish I could remember the exact words they said; their response was exactly what I needed. They relayed that I had nothing to worry about—they were having fun and enjoying a relaxed afternoon that didn't require a rushed pace. They didn't say they hadn't noticed anything, and they didn't offer their pity. Their attitude manifested in those two ways made a difference to me. Speaking tongue-in-cheek to Kevin, I thanked him for not taking a video of the staircase fiasco. His response? "Of course not! That wouldn't help anyone." As Dad was driving up with the car, I stopped and jokingly commented, "Hey, I might have crawled up a staircase, but I didn't need a helicopter to airlift me off the course! That's something." Next time, I might need the chopper, but I'm pretty sure we won't pursue this particular venue again anyway.

- Don't "overhelp." This also comes down to assumptions. Most individuals with disabilities like the opportunity to serve others when possible and to do for themselves what is in their reach. We even like giving the courtesy of holding a door open for someone. If I'm about to move a small chair, you don't have to quickly take over. It's funny because it sounds great to have everyone do everything for you, but when there are so many things you can't do for yourself, you want to be given the opportunity to do those you can. If you aren't sure if someone needs help, wait a second and see what they do. It'll likely become evident if assistance would be welcome. If you still aren't sure, just ask them and then respect their choice to receive help or not.

Advocate

Finally, you can be an advocate for the disability community. Be aware of how accessible your home and workplace are. Take initiative before people with disabilities need to speak up in order to be welcomed to participate as equals. I'm mostly in tune with my own needs, and I'm trying to learn to look out for others. A woman who attends my church has low vision and is considered legally blind. My silly brain always seems to find that to be a funny term, and I often wonder, *So what would it mean to be <u>illegally</u> blind?"* I've been helping her participate more fully in worship services by emailing her the lyrics to the songs that will be sung on an upcoming Sunday. She's able to view these on her phone, which can display the text size she needs, rather than straining to make out the words projected on the screen at the front. I know I likely miss the boat on a lot of needs, but I'm committed to watching, listening, and learning in an effort to improve conditions when I can. Everyone can work on being more observant in these ways.

I have intended for this chapter to be helpful and educational and not scolding and judgemental. I can easily believe when reading this that some would be thinking, *I can't do anything or say anything right! Robyn seems so sensitive. I can't win for trying!* I understand that people usually have good intentions, and I am far from perfect when it comes to being sensitive now or in the past about an individual's situation. Please view these suggestions as exactly that—suggestions and not hard and fast rules. Thinking before one speaks goes a long way, as does imagining how you would feel in someone else's shoes.

Sixteen
MY SUPPORT STAFF

Experiencing the steadfast love and care of Kevin and Claire is unbelievable and a beautiful reason why I continue to be filled with hope.

Handy, Helpful, Handsome Husband
Kevin's glowing report comes in the form of what I am calling "prosetry."

> Rougie is red
> Sometimes I feel blue
> Many poems rhyme
> This one tries to on the first and last lines of each stanza
> But not this stanza
>
> Husband, Lover, Best Friend, Kevin:
> You are my person
> The one I trust completely and the only one I ever want snoring beside me
> You make life better in more ways than I could imagine
> You are my sweet gift from Heaven
>
> Thank you for fruit salad and massage in the middle of our work days
> I knew then that you'd always look out for me
> Rides to the doc, sniff-testing air before I walk into a room, prayers, back rubs, and more prayers
> And so many dimmer switches!
> In 1998, how could I have possibly perceived all the ways?
>
> I can't imagine digesting news like MS without you
> You have been a rock through the ups, downs, twists, and turns
> You have learned with me, always engaged in my health care
> Thanks for patience and care with injections
> My best nurse, you show love and care in all you do

When I became irritable and mad
And gloomy, melancholy, and despondent
You noticed and felt helpless
But then you helped because you faithfully prayed for me
Soon, I emerged from my funk, a lot less sad

My diet restrictions have been hard
You're always seeking to understand the why behind it all
And you consistently find new ways to cook for me
When I lost weight, you made me pancakes
Thanks for not feeding me lard

Thank you for laughing with me
For being a reliable assistive device and for matching my slower pace
For supporting and admiring all my new learning pursuits
For building me an accessible house
God's blessings you help me see

Doting, Delightful, Dazzling Daughter

Claire Bear, you are the highlight of our sweet and happy marriage. And now I'm crying. It's just such a marvel that you exist and that we get to be your parents. I think all the other parents of the world are jealous we got you. But I'm supposed to be focusing on my health and how you've made a difference to me in that regard and not just on how you turned out.

I admire your love of cooking and making healthy meals. So many times while balancing university, you plan and make supper for our family—often with a more savoury meal for you and Dad and a custom meal for your dear mom. Your level of consideration is off the charts and is accompanied by the sacrifice of your time and energy.

I'm still amazed that you let me hang out with you and your friends and never seem embarrassed by me. The only beef I have with you is that once when I told you I was okay with you living with me while I'm married, you said you wouldn't welcome cohabitating with me when you're married. It kinda seems like a double standard, but I can let it go because I respect you so much. When I grow up, I hope to be a lot like you.

Seventeen
VISIBLE

I have spoken about *invisible* illnesses, as a lot of what I experience isn't apparent by looking at me. Thinking about my illnesses being invisible caused me to contemplate how I have experienced much that is delightfully visible. In fact, this visibility extends beyond my sense of sight. What follows is a non-exhaustive account of what my five senses have noticed.

Sight
I love seeing people looking at me and smiling. I don't mind if they give me a bit of a once-over, as I realize MS isn't completely invisible at my current stage. Using assistive devices is a clear giveaway something is up. When we had our dog and I took her for walks while driving my mobility scooter, I received many smiles from others. Indeed, it was an endearing scene: middle-aged woman driving a mobility scooter while taking an adorable small dog for a walk. I loved all those nameless encounters. And I love when people are able to move past what doesn't quite look usual to them and see the person behind it all.

Hearing
I will never tire of hearing people pray for me—especially when they first listen carefully and understand how I need intercession. I also appreciate silence and notice when people are toning down noise out of consideration for me when I experience a headache.

Touch
I can't count the number of times Kevin has massaged my legs during an especially bad episode of nerve pain, or my head, neck, and back for migraine prevention and relief. His touch feels exceptionally loving and healing. I also love hugs; I hug family, friends, Claire's friends, my pharmacy technicians from the past, my occupational therapist, my piano students, fellow church attendees …

Smell

When I can't detect fragrance from sources such as perfume, air fresheners, and scented candles, I am deeply appreciative. It means so much to me when friends and family show consideration in refraining from using fragrance when they know they'll be seeing me. I notice, and my head is thankful. And the smell of tasty food made for me is always a delight!

Taste

Mommy goes out of her way to make sure I'm included in meals we share as a larger family. She carefully quizzes me on ingredients before preparing a dish to make sure I'll be able to eat it without getting sick. She has purchased ingredients not normally placed in her shopping cart to ensure safe eating for me. I'm looking at you, leeks and lactose-free milk. My mother-in-law, Elsie, also shows consideration for my dietary needs and is conscientious in letting me know about ingredients in shared meals. Both moms often stop their food preparations to set aside a dish before Robyn-unfriendly ingredients are added.

In the early days of MS, when relapses were frequent and debilitating, we were blessed with delicious meals brought to us by family and friends. This is one example of the support and consideration we have received from our community. These moments remind me that our family isn't striving in a vacuum, and I am once again consumed with hope. Once, when I had mostly recovered from the motor relapse I'd been dealing with, I was able to prepare supper for our family. Young Claire looked at me and said, "Whose mommy made this food?" How wonderful that Claire saw the consistent care we received from our village, and what joy I had when I could respond, "*Your* mommy!"

CONCLUSION

I have a great life! It's full of joy and challenges and joy in the challenges. I live with illness and disability, and I've been treated with compassion and respect. I wanted to share my story—one full of hope and immeasurable blessing. Thanks for coming along on this adventure with me. I hope you have learned, laughed, and feel better equipped to love.

I wouldn't be able to tell a tale of hope without the foundation of my faith in Jesus Christ. I have purposely focused throughout most of the book on the practical matters of my health. The presence of the Divine in my life is intrinsic to who I am, who I have been, and who I am becoming. Through my church, I've been asked to share about my experience with illness, suffering, and disappointment. I revisited the article I wrote about chronic illness as well as the notes I used for my talks on suffering and disappointment. I came up with the content of the writing and talks years apart from each other, but I was happy to notice a consistent theme. Each time, I referenced a Bible verse that has become meaningful to me, and I'd like to end by highlighting it.

It's important to consider context when we look at passages of scripture, so before I share this verse, I'll give relevant background information. The book of Job in the Old Testament is the account of a wealthy man named Job (traditionally pronounced with a long o sound—i.e., rhymes with *robe*). He lived his life faithful to God.

One day God and Satan had a little chat, and Satan challenged God. He predicted that Job was only being obedient because of his blessed life, and if all his wealth were taken away, he would surely turn his back on God. God remained sovereign over all but allowed Satan to cause immense trouble in Job's life. Job was steadfast in his faith, not blaming God for what had happened. At the end of the book, he was blessed to an even greater degree than he was at the beginning. As the first chapter concludes, Job's initial reaction to hearing of the losses is given in the following three verses:

> At this, Job got up and tore his robe and shaved his head. Then he fell to the ground in worship and said: "Naked I came from my mother's womb, and naked I will depart. The Lord gave and the Lord has taken away; may the name of the Lord be praised." In all this, Job did not sin by charging God with wrongdoing. (Job 1:20–22)

Verse 20 tells us that he tore his robe and shaved his head. Both of these actions were common outward signs of grief. I shared verse 21 in my writing and talks. The first half of it shows us how Job recognized his mortality and the temporal nature of his life on earth, and the last half talks about God giving and God taking away and how Job chose to praise him. This three-verse passage ends with the comment, *"Job did not sin by charging God with wrongdoing,"* (Job 1:22).

Grieving and gaining perspective are both part of Job's response. I appreciate that. When we look at verse 21 in isolation, it appears that God is doing both giving and taking. However, when seen in the context of the preceding verses, it's clear that God *allowed* Satan to cause the losses in Job's life. God still had dominion, and Satan was only permitted to inflict pain in Job's life; Satan was not in control of the narrative. Job appeared to be well aware of where the pain was coming from and didn't throw blame at his Creator.

Although I relate to the grieving losses and finding perspective parts, I connect most to Job's story because I also recognize God's goodness in my life. I don't blame him for anything undesirable that has happened to me, and I praise him for everything good in my life. In fact, I praise him for the challenges too, because they have shaped who I am and are an important part of my story. I'm often told what a remarkable attitude I have. Any strength perceived in my outlook does not come from me. I'm certainly still subject to discouragement, pain, and frustration, but even more so I am hopeful. It's my desire that this manuscript not be my legacy. More than anything, I want my life to point to my God, who has showered me with immeasurable blessings.

"may the name of the Lord be praised" (Job 1:21b).

ABOUT THE AUTHOR

Robyn Derksen Olfert was born and raised in Winnipeg, Canada and has continued to make her home there. She graduated from the University of Manitoba with a Bachelor of Education and enjoyed five and a half years as a middle school teacher. Her career was interrupted when she and her husband, Kevin, joyfully welcomed their daughter, Claire. Claire's arrival also coincided with Robyn's "big diagnosis," which became a life-altering event in her family's life. Profound fatigue and subsequent disability hindered Robyn's return to full-time teaching. As the years progressed, she "collected" a total of four significant invisible illnesses along with various less impacting ones.

While in university and managing the first of these illnesses, Robyn completed her Level 10 Piano with the Royal Conservatory of Music, achieving a high standing. This has been one of her greatest accomplishments, and she has joyfully opened her home and heart to students of all ages and abilities in her small private piano studio. Teaching piano has been an ideal blend of her skills.

Robyn and her family have been members of a local church for years, and they have relished their support and community. She enjoys keeping her close extended family and loving circle of friends connected and laughing.

ACKNOWLEDGEMENTS

Kevin and Claire—You have supported me in this project from the moment I announced in July 2022 that I wanted to write a book. You never doubted me, and you encouraged me when I second-guessed myself. You kept our family fed and have taken care of me in countless ways. Thank you for believing the best about me and blessing me in the time I've dedicated to writing. What will I do now? Should I get a bigger Rubik's cube?

Derksen5—I love our family text and email groups. You've been an encouragement to me for fifty years! Thank you for your feedback, love, food, and teaching me to laugh. I'm so proud of the family I grew up in. I think we're sort of a remarkable bunch.

Jan—You support me in every single thing I pursue. You have lavished me with thoughtful gifts, including the weighted blanket I use every night to help keep my legs calm. When I had to go on medical leave, you bought me a magnet for my "retirement." For my forty-ninth birthday, you gave me a card with a picture of a woman downhill skiing, accompanied by the caption, "The word on the slopes was, she was fast." I loved those gifts. Celebrating my retirement felt heaps better than talking about medical leave, and we both know I don't do anything fast, except maybe talk. When I told you I was thinking about writing this book, you said, "One hundred percent! Yes!" You also encouraged me to go through a publisher because you never doubted it would be a success. Let's see!

All my in-laws! I love my in-laws:

> Brother—Thanks for always be willing to help out with no-nonsense medical advice, for reasonable recommendations, affirmations, and for entertaining me with your MRI impression.

> Julio—I don't have a nickname for you, but I love that you call me Tante, even if your children sometimes forget. You've

always been thoughtful and kind in your expressions of care and concern.

Mom Elsie—Thanks for raising such an amazing son! It doesn't make me happy to know you've had health challenges too. However, I have certainly benefited from your understanding of what living with a chronic illness is like.

Pearl—You're always positive and encouraging. When I shared with you that I had started writing this book, you were immediately enthusiastic and supportive, believing I'd get to the finish line.

Cheryl—Thanks for being Kevin's "best man" at our wedding and for giving me a stamp of approval when he sneaked you into our Bible study group to get to know me. I've also appreciated your willingness to answer medical questions and your genuine interest and encouragement of this book.

Val and Maren—Thank you for your help with my random grammar questions and for knowledgably answering my queries.

Patricia, I thank God for the timing of us meeting. Thank you for having the courage to tell me to let go of my darlings and then being tender with me as I mourned the loss of the superfluous words I regarded as precious. Your advice from a writer's perspective helped me make key changes to make this a book I will be happy to see published.

Uncle Randy and Auntie Jan—Our families have certainly done our share of navigating the medical world from the patient and caregiver sides. I appreciated your encouragement and insights with parts of my manuscript. Your validation of the value of this project helped me stick to it. I'm confident you have a book in you too—I can't wait to read it and would be honoured to help in any way I can.

Julia—You were the cheerleader I needed as I reached the end of writing the rough draft of this little tome. When frustrated and feeling isolated in the project, you took time to read a large portion of it and give helpful feedback. I valued your insights as a therapist and was overwhelmed with your affirmation.

The people at Word Alive Press—Thank you for holding the hand of this first-time author. I love the cover design and appreciated the help of a professional editor. It was a great learning experience and a relief to have someone else fill the role of grammar expert. Crystal, your warmth, enthusiasm, and professionalism have been a constant encouragement and tremendous help. Thanks for stepping in to be my project manager.

To all my medical practitioners—I think I struck gold with all of you. I'm taking the liberty of thanking my medical team, as health is the theme of this book. They may not have all been directly involved with the book, but they've made a difference to my healthcare, and that sure seems relevant.

> My MS neurologists:
> Dr. Melanson—You were kind, personable, professional, and knowledgeable when it came to my healthcare. What a great first MS doc to have!
>
> Dr. Marriott—Thank you for your expertise and working with me for years. I will always appreciate how you advocated for me with my application for the Disability Tax Credit.
>
> Dr. Saab—I'm hoping to be under your care for years to come! You've been easy to talk to, and I have already appreciated many of your insights. I'm overwhelmed with gratitude that you took the time to read my manuscript and give me feedback.
>
> Dr. Tadrous—You have been a wonderful family doctor for me. I appreciate your sincere concern and care. You're knowledgeable, have had unique and important insights, have been a great listener, and have always taken a genuine interest in my health and life.
>
> Andrew—I love telling people about my orthotist. No one seems to know who you people are, but I know you've increased the quality of my life. I love how we can laugh at appointments, how you cheer me on when I say I'm going to get jacked and need a size adjustment on my AFO, and that you cheerfully answer all my questions. I appreciated your input about the

discussion of AFOs in this book. I love your enthusiasm for my cartoon animal drawings, but despite your wishes, this volume will not be an illustrated one. I'll have to send you another thank you card with an animal wearing one of my AFOs.

Chad—Somehow our thirty-minute appointments always take an hour. When I asked you about that, you said it was "physio and coffee." There's nothing awkward about having my cottage buddy and lifelong friend as my physiotherapist. You're consistently positive and enthusiastic about me and put up with me appointment after appointment when it's clear I am rubbish at doing my exercise homework. Growing up with two sisters, I loved having you as an honorary brother.

Bev and Dan—You have been dear friends and mentors. It was a privilege to be your patient, Bev. You went the extra mile with me—literally; I can remember at least one house call. Compassion is an adjective, which doesn't do you two justice. Thank you both for your prayers over the last three decades.

Finally, I have a few words of thanks for some key players in my little drama. I want to give a big shout out to my body! After all, without you, Body, I wouldn't have had a book to write. I also wouldn't have learned how to be more gracious, compassionate, understanding, relatable, and God-fearing. And I always appreciate another reason to enjoy a laugh, of course!

Thank you, Right Leg. I'm sorry about that time at hippotherapy when I told the physiotherapist you don't do anything for yourself. That's not true. You do lots. I know it's not your fault you can't do all the leg tricks out there. Without you, I'd have no steps to count.

Thank you, Left Leg. You're so gracious and happy to do the jobs assigned to you and never flex on Right Leg that you're a little more athletic than her. And you never act jealous when Right Foot and Ankle get another new fashionable AFO.

Thank you, Immune System. You may be attacking my nervous system, but I appreciate the restraint you've shown in staying away from other organ systems.

Thank you, CNS. I like you, Brain. You're fun to do things with. I'm glad you've let me take you cubing and map-gazing. I like you too, Spinal Cord. You're a busy little dude, sending millions of messages each day, so my body parts know when to move and when to feel sensations and when to flex their abnormally brisk reflexes.

My dear Myelin, I know you try hard to protect me, and I'm sorry you've sometimes been under attack. I want you to know I don't blame you; I know you continue to do your best and didn't actually give your consent to the battle scars you've gained.

Thank you, Head. I'm sorry you hurt a lot, but don't we have fun when you're having a good day? I like taking you on learning adventures.

Thank you, Liver, for consistently getting amazing report cards, even after processing my medications. I know you didn't sign up for this, but you show up to work every day.

Thank you, Elimination Systems. I'm sorry for complaining about you so often. Truly, I am grateful you help me take the trash out, even if it takes extra time.

Thank you, Digestive System. I'm committed to finding ways we can work well together. I'll do my best not to poison you with gluten, lactose, onions, or garlic.

Thank you, Heart and Lungs. You're never late for your shifts and have kept me going for over fifty years non-stop. You're the unsung heroes.

Thank you, Appendix. You've drawn absolutely no attention to yourself. Keep it up!

Thank you, my Creator, who made this shell I inhabit. The human body is a marvel and points to the Intelligence behind its design. I'm can't wait to see what you've been working on for Human Body 2.0, Eternal Edition. Will I run as fast as a cheetah? Will I fly like my name so wants me to? Whatever you have in store, just being with you will be the best part.

www.ingramcontent.com/pod-product-compliance
Lightning Source LLC
LaVergne TN
LVHW051119080426
835510LV00018B/2117